The Maharishi Effect

The Maharishi Effect

A Personal Journey Through the Movement That Transformed American Spirituality

Geoff Gilpin

Jeremy P. Tarcher/Penguin

a member of Penguin Group (USA) Inc.

New York

JEREMY P. TARCHER/PENGUIN
Published by the Penguin Group
Penguin Group (USA) Inc., 375 Hudson Street, New York, New York 10014, USA · Penguin Group
(Canada), 90 Eglinton Avenue East, Suite 700, Toronto, Ontario M4P 2Y3 Canada (a division of Pearson
Penguin Canada Inc.) · Penguin Books Ltd, 80 Strand, London WC2R 0RL, England · Penguin Ireland,
25 St Stephen's Green, Dublin 2, Ireland (a division of Penguin Books Ltd) · Penguin Group (Australia),
250 Camberwell Road, Camberwell, Victoria 3124, Australia (a division of Pearson Australia Group
Pty Ltd) · Penguin Books India Pvt Ltd, 11 Community Centre, Panchsheel Park, New Delhi–110 017,
India · Penguin Group (NZ), Cnr Airborne and Rosedale Roads, Albany, Auckland 1310, New Zealand
(a division of Pearson New Zealand Ltd) · Penguin Books (South Africa) (Pty) Ltd, 24 Sturdee Avenue,
Rosebank, Johannesburg 2196, South Africa

Penguin Books Ltd, Registered Offices: 80 Strand, London WC2R 0RL, England

Most Tarcher/Penguin books are available at special quantity discounts for bulk purchase for sales promo-
tions, premiums, fund-raising, and educational needs. Special books or book excerpts also can be created to
fit specific needs. For details, write Penguin Group (USA) Inc. Special Markets, 375 Hudson Street,
New York, NY 10014.

Library of Congress Cataloging-in-Publication Data

Gilpin, Geoff.
The Maharishi effect : a personal journey through the movement that transformed American spirituality /
by Geoff Gilpin.
p.   cm.
Includes bibliographical references and index.
ISBN 1-58542-507-9
1. Transcendental Meditation.   2. Mahesh Yogi, Maharishi—Teachings.   3. Gilpin, Geoff.   4. Maharishi
International University—Alumni and alumnae.   I. Title.

BF637.T68G55   2006   2006044625
58'.9—dc21

Printed in the United States of America
1   3   5   7   9   10   8   6   4   2

Book design by Chris Welch

While the author has made every effort to provide accurate telephone numbers and Internet addresses at the
time of publication, neither the publisher nor the author assumes any reponsibility for errors, or for changes
that occur after publication. Further, the publisher does not have any control over and does not assume any
responsibility for author or third-party websites or their content.

MAY 2 3 2007

For Sarah,

who taught me that love is stronger than fear

Contents

Preface

America in the twenty-first century is a spiritual wonderland. If you're starting out on the sacred path, you can probably find a church or guru or tradition that feels like home. If you're not a joiner, you can build your own enlightenment out of countless revelations and cosmologies.

It certainly wasn't like that when I was growing up in the fifties. Spiritual people could be Protestant, Catholic, or Jewish . . . and that was about it. Like so much else, however, America's inner landscape shifted forever in the 1960s. Adventurous seekers dug up the esoteric and occult and made them popular. Eastern teachers arrived bearing unfamiliar wisdom. It was a great time to explore the inner planes.

One of the most important influences on the spiritual revolution of the sixties was Transcendental Meditation. TM is a simple meditation technique popularized by the Indian guru Maharishi Mahesh Yogi. Thanks to Maharishi's brilliant marketing, millions of Americans learned that meditation is a powerful and effective tool. Most of them didn't stick with the TM technique itself, but many continued to explore spiritual alternatives. The cultural explosion that followed—the human potential movement and the New Age—began with Maharishi as much as anybody.

I was one of the thronging masses who learned TM back in the day. I wasn't content to sit with my eyes closed, however; I wanted to find out if Maharishi had anything else to offer. My curiosity led me into the Movement, the worldwide organization that Maharishi established to teach TM and bring enlightenment to the planet. I spent five years in the Movement, from 1973 to 1978, as a hanger-on, volunteer, and student at Maharishi International University.

When I left, it was for the usual reasons. I got a job, a wife, a house in the suburbs—the whole nine yards. I continued to meditate, but I was out of the Movement loop for two decades.

Then I went back. In part, I wanted to reconnect with the spiritual life I'd neglected since young adulthood. I'd also heard of some unsettling developments in the Movement and I was curious to find out what was going on firsthand. There might have been a small midlife crisis in there somewhere as well.

Starting in 1999, I made periodic visits to the American headquarters of the TM Movement in Fairfield, Iowa. I got in touch with old friends and I made a number of new acquaintances at various levels of the organization. I met Movement leaders, former members who left for a variety of reasons, and the ordinary but wonderful Iowans who look on in bemusement. For a few months in 2001, I took a local apartment and lived in the town that's at the center of America's spiritual revolution.

Before you turn the page and begin the journey, I'd like to address a couple of questions you might have along the way.

This book is a work of nonfiction. The people, conversations, and events are real. In some cases, I've concealed the identities of real people through the use of fictitious names, locations, and other personal details. I did this for anybody who specifically requested anonymity. In situations where there was any doubt, I tried to err on the side of privacy.

In a few instances, I've combined two or more real people into a single, composite portrait. This was one of the methods I used to ensure privacy when it was necessary. I also relied on composite characters to streamline the narrative and keep the cast to a manageable size.

Some of the events in this book appear outside the chronological order in which they occurred. Again, this was in the interest of streamlining the narrative.

When I was writing this book, my goal was to present the facts in a compelling manner. Whenever possible, I relied on the personal testimony of multiple witnesses, reliable publications, video and audio recordings, and written notes. I've done everything I could to eliminate errors. In the end, however, a lot of what you're about to read came out of my own observations and memories. I can't promise they're perfect, but I can assure you that they work in the service of truth.

Geoff Gilpin

March 2006

Chapter 1

Maharishi's Final Warning

My friends levitate. The whole gang—Jamie, Doug, Beth—zoom through the air like helicopters. Anyway, that's what they called it—"flying," "levitation," and so forth. I know better because I peeked.

This was twenty-five years ago when levitating was the biggest secret in the Transcendental Meditation Movement. The flyers didn't have the Golden Dome back then, so they made do in the first-floor lounge of my dormitory. They hung sheets over the windows and told everyone else to keep out. The cloak-and-dagger stuff was pretty lame because all I had to do was walk down the stairs, open the door, and look in.

Judging by the sounds I heard as I snuck down the stairs in my socks, levitation is a lot like an orgy.

"Ooooooo!"

"Eeee-yaaaa!"

Barring group sex, I was hoping to see a bunch of people hovering in the air the way the rumor mill described it. (Sample rumor: "Air traffic controllers will lose their jobs unless they learn to direct people instead of airplanes.")

"Ahhh-ahhh-AHHH!"

When I got to the bottom of the stairs, I saw that somebody had tacked up a picture of Maharishi, our guru, on the door of the men's lounge. His gaze surprised me with a pang of dread. If the stories were true and he's an incarnation of God, then he knew that I was about to commit the biggest no-no in the Movement. I was dripping sweat as I cracked the door and peered in from the shadows.

A bunch of guys were sitting in the lotus position on the floor, which was covered wall-to-wall with foam mats. Jamie was quivering all over and yelping like he was getting a root canal. The guys around him were bouncing up and down on their butts and giggling furiously.

After much twitching, Jamie went airborne. He pushed himself off the ground with his knees and bounced forward in a series of short hops—thud, thud, thud—landing on his butt with a goofy grin.

In my five years with the Movement, I'd seen the heights of devotion and the depths of superstition. I'd been through hope and despair, love and paranoia, soaring excitement and grinding boredom. By then, it wasn't much of a surprise to learn that my best friend had a secret life, bouncing up and down on foam.

The thing that bugged me, as I stood in the shadows watching the happy faces go up and down, was the knowledge that each one of them believed without question that he was flying through the air under his own power like Superman. I knew these guys, and I knew the Movement. If Maharishi said butt-bouncing on foam rubber was magic, a miracle, a paranormal suspension of Newtonian physics, then it was. Period.

So did you ever learn to fly?" my wife asked.

"No. The flying course was still new when I left the Movement in '78. It was just a few people at first."

We were sitting at the dinner table in our house in rural Wisconsin about twenty minutes outside Madison, the state capital. I spread butter on the corn we got from the neighboring farm and thought about the Movement I'd left two decades earlier.

"Maharishi changed the policy later and opened up the flying course to the general public. It was kind of a shock. Levitation used to be a big secret, like the stealth bomber technology of the Movement, and then suddenly they were taking out big ads and giving press conferences. They had this PR event called the Olympics of Yogic Flying."

Sarah took a bite of mashed potato and gave me a doubtful look.

"I saw it on TV. There were guys wearing number jerseys bouncing around in the lotus position and a referee following them with a measuring tape.

"Everybody in the Movement was a flyer by then. If I'd stayed, I could have learned it for a fraction of what it costs now. But I'd moved on."

"Any regrets?" Sarah asked, draining her wine glass.

"Oh . . . lots." We both smiled.

After dinner I went upstairs to my office to put in some work time before bed. I was the co-owner of a small computer services firm in Madison. We did documentation, training, online help systems, consulting—pretty much everything except the actual hardware and software.

I settled in at the PC to download the latest version of RightSize!, the product of Executive Software Decisions, my client of the moment. The purpose of RightSize!—at least the official reason for its existence—was to guide corporate executives through the downsizing process.

"RightSize! offers executives accurate corporate restructuring support using proprietary algorithms developed by leading corporate restructuring support experts."

"It lets them cover their asses," explained Gabe, the company president, when I visited his office in Chicago. "Say they make the wrong decision and close the plant in Wichita instead of the plant in Omaha and the company loses a million bucks. They get hauled in front of the board of directors and they can say 'I did what the algorithms told me.' It gives them ammunition for keeping their job."

Gabe himself wrote the parts of the RightSize! software that actually made decisions. The interface—the buttons and graphs and dialog boxes you see when you're working with the program—came from a guy in

Nizhni Novgorod named Boris. Gabe discovered him on a business tour of the former Soviet Union, where programmers work for much less than their American counterparts.

Boris was actually pretty good. He could write quality code for Microsoft Windows. However, he had some peculiar assumptions about the software interface experience.

I started the program and the RightSize! logo appeared against a background of question marks and dollar signs. I noticed that Boris had changed all the controls on the main toolbar. The graphic on one button showed a picture of a dog's head—a terrier, apparently. Another button had a picture of a mop and pail. I couldn't figure out the graphic on a third button, but it might have been a comb going through somebody's hair.

It looked like Boris scrapped a bunch of his code from the last version and started over, which meant that I had to toss a lot of my own work and learn the program from scratch. Then I had ten days to create the text for all the program's screens, write the manual, and make a training video.

I read the text file where Boris left cryptic clues about his intentions.

"To make executive decision, please click button 'Decide.'"

Sure enough, the Decide button was the one with the mop. I clicked it. Nothing. I clicked again. The screen froze. The keyboard and mouse wouldn't respond. The hard drive let out a morbid squeal and my computer gave up and died.

I wanted to cry.

Late one afternoon in May of 1999, I came home from the office I shared with my two business partners in downtown Madison. I put down my briefcase, kissed my wife, and rummaged through the pile of mail on the kitchen counter. I saw a flyer with a familiar gold and pastel color scheme.

MAHARISHI'S FINAL WARNING TO THE UNITED STATES

Huh? This was the first Movement flyer I'd seen with a warning.

"The horrors of war being witnessed in Yugoslavia have created fear in the hearts of everyone everywhere."

Yugoslavia? How odd. During all my years in the Movement, I'd never heard Maharishi comment on current events. He was too cosmic.

"The issue is the trend of the U.S. to deal with conflicts through destruction—if somebody doesn't agree with you, then you send them to heaven. If this destructive trend continues, in the next generation there will be no United States. . . . Imagine if bombs began to fall on Washington, D.C., and to destroy the high-rises of the money markets of New York."

I frowned and put the flyer down. It looked like all the other unsolicited mail I got from the Movement, but the violent words seemed to come from a strange source. It made me wonder what was going on.

For a second I felt the queasy, superstitious dread that I thought I had left behind ages ago. What if Maharishi really is God? Would he know if the bombs were about to fall? I looked around at the familiar objects in my kitchen. No, he isn't God.

"Would you like tuna fish casserole for dinner?"

"Oh . . . yeah. That would be perfect." Bless you, Sarah.

While my wife opened a can of tuna, I continued with Maharishi's final warning. He railed against NATO, the United Nations, American foreign policy, and Bill Clinton. He predicted it would all end in flames.

It was more like the Book of Revelation than the peace and love and Transcendental Meditation I remembered. In fact, it was so totally out of character that I wondered if it came from Maharishi at all. How old was he? Somewhere in his eighties? Maybe he had Alzheimer's.

I thought of my old friends and wondered if any of them were still in the Movement. Last I heard, Doug was a starving artist in Europe. Beth might still be around. She used to work at our alma mater—Maharishi International University in Fairfield, Iowa—doing publicity or fundraising or something. Her byline turned up in Movement newsletters from time to time.

I climbed the stairs to my office and rummaged through the filing cabinet where I kept the Movement's junk mail. Lord knows they'd sent enough of it over the years. Maharishi's presses churned out whole libraries of books, magazines, newsletters, and brochures, much of it expensively printed on heavy paper with a lot of gold leaf.

Ninety percent of it went into the trash, but I still had a huge collection. *The Age of Enlightenment News. Golden Domes Quarterly.* Various announcements of new programs and opportunities to donate money. I kept anything with pictures of old friends or places with good memories. I had a separate Tyvek envelope for anything funny or outrageous.

I was going through this envelope when I found Beth's name in a couple of the Movement's glossy publications. I pulled out an article about Maharishi's Endowment Fund for Perpetual World Peace.

"World's Wealthiest Called Upon," it read, appealing to the world's billionaires to support Maharishi's fund. "They should give 1% of their wealth to this Endowment Fund, thereby protecting the other 99% of their wealth." The money would go to support a group of 40,000 Yogic Flyers who would levitate together and generate the 'Maharishi Effect,' a cosmic wave that would bury war, crime, terrorism, poverty, and suffering for eternity.

I tried to imagine forty thousand people—a fifth of the population of nearby Madison, Wisconsin—seated in the lotus position on a sea of foam mats, hopping up and down on their butts and shrieking like jaybirds.

After failing at that, I tried to imagine Beth's voice, with its ever-so-slight southern accent—saying things like "it is the responsibility of the world's wealthiest to give one percent of their wealth." I failed again. I could only hear her saying things she might actually say, such as:

> "I really like the Incredible String Band!"
> or
> "I don't think I love you anymore, Geoff."

Good, warm, big-hearted Beth Adair. Twenty years is way too long to go without hearing from someone who was so important to you. I wondered if she was still working at MIU. I phoned directory assistance for Fairfield, Iowa, and got the number.

"Maharishi University of Management," said a flat male voice.

They changed the name. Typical.

"How may I direct your call?"

"I'd like to speak with Beth Adair."

A pause.

"Are you a relative of Beth Adair?"

"No. I'm a friend. An alumnus. Beth and I graduated from MIU in 1978."

Silence.

"Beth Adair is no longer at this facility."

He made it sound like an iron gate falling shut.

I hung up the phone, sat back in my desk chair, and wondered what happened. In my day, the person who answered the phone was usually some blissed-out eighteen-year-old who meant well but had a difficult time navigating the campus directory. This guy sounded more professional, but cold as ice. And when did they start calling the place a "facility"?

Sarah appeared at my office door and announced dinner. Over our second helping of tuna fish casserole, I showed her Maharishi's final warning and asked for an opinion.

"Well, I actually agree with some of this," she said. "But as it goes on it gets more and more off the wall.

"It reminds me of tracts that street corner preachers hand out—the ones that say that Armageddon is coming and all the believers will go up to heaven in the rapture while all the unbelievers stay behind and suffer. You still have friends in that group, don't you?"

"Yes."

The best friends I ever had, I thought. A long-lost memory came back to me: all of us sitting in the common room of our dormitory, huddled under an igloo of blankets.

In the frigid cold winter of 1977, the heat went out on the MIU campus. No furnace, no hot water for days. During one blizzard, when it was too cold to venture outside, the kitchen staff packed up boxes of bread and peanut butter and strawberry cheesecake and pulled them to the dormitories on sleds. It was like a rescue party arriving at a stranded Antarctic research station.

Beth made cocoa in her hot pot and passed it out in Styrofoam cups. Jamie unpacked slabs of cheesecake from the snow-covered cardboard box. There were candles and body heat under the blankets. Somebody played a guitar.

"I guess if I had friends in a group that was handing out literature like that . . ." Sarah said as she gave me a second helping of tuna casserole, "well, I guess I'd be concerned."

I contemplated one of the peas on my plate and pushed it around with my fork. As a favor, Sarah made tuna fish casserole using my mom's classic fifties recipe that includes a whole bag of potato chips. I've eaten this meal for forty-five years, with the exception of the five years I spent in the Movement eating brown rice and tofu.

Sarah gave me the smile that always made me feel peaceful.

"Honey . . ." I said, "I think I need to go back to Iowa for a visit."

Chapter 2

The Movement

So what do you know about this guy?" Sarah asked as she guided our red convertible out of the neighborhood onto the highway that led back into the Movement.

"Well, he's supposed to be God—an incarnation of Shiva, the Destroyer. He's destroying the ignorance and suffering of the human race. He's the highest form of consciousness on the planet."

"That's it?"

I smiled. "It's what's important, at least if you're a believer. But I guess most people think of him as the Beatles guru. That's how he became famous."

Before 1967, hardly anyone outside India knew what a guru was. Then the Beatles went searching for Eastern wisdom and met Maharishi. He turned up everywhere—on every magazine cover and talk show, it seemed—and we all learned what an Indian holy man looked and sounded like. Other gurus followed once the market opened up, but none of them were as successful or influential as the original.

It's the same thing with meditation. Until the late sixties, it was virtually unknown in the West outside monasteries and a few isolated yoga groups. Then Maharishi appeared and introduced TM as everyman's path to inner peace. Nowadays a significant chunk of Americans practice meditation of some sort.

"Maharishi's an icon," I said. "He's a big part of the sixties counterculture, but he's more than that. He really changed Western society forever.

"It's funny, though. He kind of gets lost in his own legend. Everybody in the Movement has some bizarre story about him. They saw him floating in the clouds or two people saw him in different cities at the same time. You know that there's a human being in there somewhere, but it's hard to make him out.

"I'm not even sure what his real name is. His first name is Mahesh—everybody agrees on that—but you hear different last names."

"Maharishi is a title?" asked Sarah.

"Yeah. It means 'great seer' in Sanskrit.

"His early life is pretty vague. I've seen dates of birth ranging from 1911 to 1918."

I paused for a bit and took a map from Sarah's collection. She'd stocked the convertible with state maps, county maps, atlases, and directories of parks, hiking trails, and roadside cafés. My wife is the most geographically competent person I've ever known.

I found us on the Wisconsin map driving southwest from Madison, the state capital, on our way to the Mississippi River and Iowa. The urban sprawl thinned out as we rode past corn fields and cow pastures.

"He hardly ever talks about his personal life, but I read an interview where he mentioned going to college. He apparently went to the University of Allahabad and studied physics.

"I don't know if he graduated or not, but his scientific career didn't last long in any case. The big turning point for him came when he met a famous holy man called Guru Dev. Guru Dev was one of the most important religious leaders in India at the time and by all accounts a very impressive person."

According to his biography,[1] the young Mahesh joined Guru Dev's monastery at Jyotir Math in northern India sometime in the early 1940s. He started calling himself Brahmachari, which means celibate.

"He lived in the monastery for about a decade working as Guru Dev's secretary," I told Sarah. "According to Movement lore, he became enlightened by devoting himself to his master day and night."

I took another peek at the map and followed the line of Highway 151 out of Wisconsin into Iowa.

"This is the route we used to take in the seventies," I said.

There was a small contingent of Wisconsinites in the student body at Maharishi International University. We made the trip back and forth in my buddy Doug Bishop's old beater Chevy. There was Doug from Green Bay, his girlfriend Trisha from Milwaukee, me, and others who came and went.

Doug and Trisha were the Movement's odd couple. In a religious sect that values calm and decorum above all, Doug's volume level was striking. He wore loud Hawaiian shirts and he blasted his stereo. He had extreme opinions on everything and he swore frequently in a booming baritone.

Trisha, by contrast, was prim and, as we used to say back then, "totally sold out to Maharishi." She was the sort of person that Doug would have tossed off as a "bliss ninny" if she hadn't been so much fun.

On our first trip to Iowa, she gave me a present—two framed photographs, one of Maharishi and one of Guru Dev. When we got to Iowa I discovered that practically every room on the campus of Maharishi University had the same two photographs hanging on the wall.

"There's a Pizzeria Magnifico!" announced Sarah as we drove through downtown Platteville, about thirty minutes from the Mississippi. We were both hungry enough to stop. We ate breadsticks and sipped iced tea as I told Sarah about the death of Guru Dev.

"He died very suddenly in 1953. Maharishi was still just Brahmachari Mahesh, a monk without a master. He left Guru Dev's monastery and went into seclusion for a year or so.

"There's a famous story about his re-entry into the world," I told Sarah. "He decided to go on a pilgrimage to holy sites in southern India. So he traveled around and he wound up in a temple devoted to the goddess Lakshmi. Lakshmi's the goddess of wealth and good fortune, but she's also Mother Divine, the goddess of everything.

"So he was in the temple and he had a vision or revelation of some kind. He realized that his mission in life was to spread Guru Dev's message of salvation to the whole world. He would cease to be a simple monk and become the teacher who would bring enlightenment to the entire human race.

"According to the story, he asked Mother Divine if this was possible and she said no, but he decided to go ahead anyway."

An amused look came over Sarah's face, as if she were contemplating the sort of person who would ask God's opinion and then blow it off.

Our deep-dish spinach pizza arrived and we took a break from the saga to eat. I looked at my watch and calculated that we'd arrive on campus by late afternoon. They'd be trooping into the dining hall about now, heading for the steam tables and filling their plates with brown rice, curried tofu, and broccoli sautéed in clarified butter.

I stared at the gooey slab on my plate. *Tamasic,* I thought, a Sanskrit word that probably hadn't occurred to me since I left Fairfield. Impure.

The Movement divides everything—people, places, food, clothing, ideas—into pure and impure. The dividing line is always there and you always know what side you're on. Some people never left the Movement campus because the outside world was, as we used to say, "nothing but mud."

I looked around at the dimly lit interior of Pizzeria Magnifico. The neon beer signs; the football game on the TV behind the bar; the faux stained glass window, illuminated by a low-watt bulb, with an intricate mosaic of red and white plastic pieces molded into the shape of Bucky Badger—every last bit of it as tamasic as hell.

Big muddy river ahead!" announced Sarah as the Mississippi came into view. We left Wisconsin and drove onto the bridge that took us over the wide brown river into Dubuque. We went on for a while in silence until the river valley rose and broadened into the farmlands that continue to Fairfield. Then I picked up the tale of my former guru.

"After his vision in the temple, he spent a couple of years in the mid-fifties traveling around India on a lecture tour. He dropped the Brahmachari from his name and started calling himself Maharishi Mahesh Yogi. He also started using the term Transcendental Meditation."

The origins of TM are obscure. According to the Movement party line, it comes from a tradition of masters that goes back to the beginning of time. The basic technique is certainly nothing new—it involves mental repetition of a *mantra,* a sacred sound, word, or phrase. Mantra meditation in one form or another has been around in India for thousands of years.

Wherever its origins, the trademarked TM technique is unique in the way it's taught and practiced. Unlike Zen or other forms of meditation, there's no concentration on the mantra. Conscious effort of any sort ruins the effect.

"It's supposed to be so easy that anybody can learn it," I said. "There aren't any lifestyle requirements; you don't have to be celibate or a vegetarian or anything. It's meditation for householders and not monks.

"Maharishi wanted everybody in the world to do TM. That was his plan to enlighten the human race. He was fairly successful in India, but that was just the beginning."

The newly fledged guru toured Asia in the late fifties and made his first trip to America in 1959. He spent the sixties traveling around the world lecturing and teaching TM nonstop.

"The world outside India wasn't too receptive to him at first," I said. "You can imagine him coming to the United States during the Eisenhower administration and giving a lecture about Cosmic Consciousness. The audience was pretty small.

"That all changed when the Beatles appeared."

It was in London in 1967. The counterculture was in full bloom and young Brits were discovering Eastern religion. Maharishi's following in England was probably larger than anywhere outside of India.

The Beatles learned of Maharishi through George's wife, Patti, who, like her husband, was fascinated by Indian religion. The group went to hear the guru speak in person at a London hotel in August. By coincidence, this lecture was Maharishi's last appearance in public.

The Fab Four were so impressed that they departed for a TM course in Wales two days after the London meeting. Early in 1968, they left England to join Maharishi at his Academy of Meditation in Shankaracharya Nagar in India. Along with their wives and assorted camp followers, they were joined by the cream of the pop world at the time—the Rolling Stones, Donovan, Mia Farrow, and the Beach Boys. Unfortunately, the honeymoon didn't last.

"Oh, this is something I actually know about," said Sarah. My wife can answer just about any question on world history or geography. She also has good chunks of the arts and sciences covered. Pop culture, however, is invisible to her. "The Beatles got mad and left because Maharishi put the moves on Mia Farrow."

"Who knows what really happened?" I shrugged. "There are a bunch of different accounts. Of course, if you're a true believer, it's inconceivable that he would do something like that. He's a celibate monk. Period.

"In any case, it was all over fairly quickly. The Beatles left India and ended their relationship with Maharishi. It was probably inevitable. They were young and impetuous and they got caught up in Maharishi's charisma, but they hardly knew him when they went off to India. They would have become disillusioned sooner or later.

"At any rate, they didn't have to stick around long to make Maharishi a celebrity."

TM went from nothing to global fad within a couple of years. To meet the demand, Maharishi trained thousands of his most devoted followers as TM initiators. (It's hard to say exactly how many, but it's a pretty big number. I've seen estimates between 10,000 and 30,000). By the mid-seventies, most American cities of any size had a storefront TM center and a listing for "Meditation, Transcendental" in the yellow pages.

"Maharishi was marketing Eastern spirituality like hamburgers. People back then called TM the McDonald's of meditation. McMantra . . . that sort of thing. Kind of generic and bland, but everywhere."

"I remember seeing TM posters all over the place at Kent State," said Sarah, who studied history there in the early seventies.

"That's how I got started," I said. "I saw one of those posters in Green Bay in 1973. They were everywhere. Everything was totally standardized. The poster had a space at the bottom where the local TM teacher could write in the time and place for the free public lecture."

I told her that the lectures took standardization to the level of the Stepford Wives. TM initiators in Wisconsin and Australia and everywhere else read the same script in the same soothing tones using the same hand gestures.

It was an unusual strategy for the age of "do your own thing," but it worked brilliantly. The McDonald's of meditation brought in people who wouldn't dream of entering a Buddhist shrine or a Hindu temple. Mr. and Mrs. Middle America could go to a TM lecture and see a clean-cut guy in a suit and tie talk about the ways that meditation could improve their lives.

What's more, they started the practice in droves. It was a watershed, a major cultural transformation.

"I'm not sure how many people got initiated," I told Sarah. "I've heard that the Movement's records are pretty spotty, especially in the early days. Maharishi himself may not even know. It's a huge number, though. Somewhere in the millions."

Chapter 3

A Simple Technique

There's a street in a seedy neighborhood in Green Bay where every building is a tavern. I used to go there to meditate. Late at night, after the bars had closed, I'd walk up and down the street chanting a holy word I found in a book:

"Ooooooommmmm."

I liked the results—a mild, floaty trance that replaced the noise in my head with blessed calm. After an hour or so, when everything on the street of taverns seemed perfectly beautiful, I stopped chanting and walked back through dark neighborhoods to the run-down apartment I shared with a drug dealer and a receiver of stolen goods.

My roommates did not appreciate my new interest in Eastern mysticism. One day, as I was placing a small figurine of Buddha on the stereo cabinet next to the box with the flashing lights, my roommate Todd looked up from the floor and pointed a finger.

"Is that the guy you're giving up pot for?" he asked sarcastically.

"Yeah, I guess."

Todd narrowed his brow and stared at me before snorting and shaking his head.

"You weird fucker," he said, getting back on his hands and knees to pick through the shag carpet and look for the tab of mescaline he'd dropped the day before.

Todd was understandably disappointed in me. Our relationship was based on mutual enthusiasm for controlled substances, and he was losing a stalwart doping buddy to a foreign religion. My motive—boredom—would have been incomprehensible to him, so I didn't bother telling him that I was sick of getting high.

My roommate was so charmed with the innocent pleasures of dope and Grand Funk Railroad that he failed to notice the death and embalming of the sixties. True, Todd and I could still scandalize the odd passerby with our long hair, but only because we lived in northern Wisconsin. By the time the sixties finally reached Green Bay, it was well into the chronological seventies. Disco and leisure suits would soon stalk the land.

The Revolution never came. LSD didn't transform global consciousness. The world was getting duller every day, and, as far as I could tell, it would never get interesting again.

One evening I was walking down the street of taverns chanting my second-hand mantra when I noticed a poster in the window of the Crystal Locomotive Saloon.

FREE PUBLIC LECTURE
TRANSCENDENTAL MEDITATION

I stopped chanting and examined the poster. It featured a picture of a dark-skinned man with long gray hair and a full beard wearing a white robe and an expression of calm authority.

An Indian holy man! Here in Green Bay! Maybe the seventies wouldn't be a total loss after all.

The lecture was in a downtown bank—far enough from my apartment that I'd need to bum a ride or take the bus. I could usually rely on Todd for transportation, but I knew that he'd balk at this one. I gave him my best sales pitch.

"TM is just like acid," I said, repeating a rumor that was going around at the time. "It's a natural high. Anytime you want you can just sit down and close your eyes and go on a trip."

At the time, I felt a little guilty for leading Todd on like that. But I wasn't going to get a ride by tempting him with release from the wheel of karma.

On the designated afternoon, we got in Todd's van and drove downtown. The lecture was in a windowless, fluorescent-lit conference room—the least mystical place in the least mystical city in the world.

I was disappointed to learn that Maharishi himself wouldn't be present. Instead, there were two of his emissaries—Bob and Harry, polite, soft-spoken young men wearing what the Movement refers to as "the attire of an initiator." Suit and tie. Hair off the ears and collar.

As we walked in, Harry welcomed us in a voice barely above a whisper. He handed us a couple of brochures and we joined the dozen or so people seated in institutional chairs. There were a few hippies like Todd and me and a mix of student types and nondescript older folks.

I paged through the brochure, which contained scientific charts describing the benefits of TM. Lower blood pressure. Less tobacco and alcohol use. Reduced galvanic skin conductivity, which I took to be a desirable thing.

What about enlightenment? Union with the divine? Freedom from the bondage of the karmic wheel?

Bob took the podium and spoke in a voice that, while audible, seldom varied in pitch or volume.

"Transcendental Meditation, as taught by Maharishi Mahesh Yogi, is a simple, natural, effortless technique for attaining deep rest."

He talked a lot about using TM to relieve stress. As a visual aid, he drew a tic-tac-toe grid on a blackboard by the podium.

"This is your nervous system," he explained. Then he drew a small spiral at the intersection of two lines.

"This is stress," he said. Then he took an eraser, which is like TM, and rubbed out the spiral to return the nervous system to its pristine, stress-free state.

When it was over, a few people from the audience went up to Bob with personal questions. I waited until they were finished before approaching him.

"Does TM produce enlightenment?" I asked point blank.

"Yes," he said with a furtive look. "TM is the fastest path to enlightenment. Maharishi says that TM leads to enlightenment within five to eight years."

He said it in a bland, bored way, as if enlightenment were a mere afterthought compared to the wonders of galvanic skin conductivity. I asked him about union with the divine and release from the karmic wheel.

"TM will give you the results you want," he said.

On the ride back home, I weighed TM against the other spiritual paths I could follow. Bob's lecture didn't have much to do with the Eastern mysticism I'd read about in books like *Autobiography of a Yogi* and *Be Here Now*. Nevertheless, he and Harry had something—a kind of calm detachment that seemed like the sort of behavior you'd expect from an enlightened person. And they both had a knowing air about them, as if they were on to a lot more than they were willing to talk about.

For all the blood pressure and skin conductivity, the TM lecture was the closest I'd come to a gathering of Eastern mystics. There just wasn't much else out there. Todd and I might cruise on the fumes of the counterculture for another year or so . . . but then what? Law school? Heroin? Plastics?

I wanted enlightenment, and all the books I'd read about meditation and spiritual development agreed on one thing: you can only go so far by yourself. At some point, if you really want to evolve, you need to find a teacher. I wished that Bob was a Zen master or a Tibetan lama or just about anyone except a guy in a suit with a canned spiel. However, in Green Bay in 1973, Transcendental Meditation was the only game in town.

—

The year I began TM, the year everybody else calls 1973, is known in the Movement as Maharishi's Year of the World Plan. We know that from the man himself.

Every year at the beginning of January, Maharishi "goes into silence." He goes into his room and shuts the door and, according to Movement lore, "communes with Mother Divine."

He comes out on January 12th—his birthday—and delivers an address to the global faithful over his satellite TV network. In this speech, Maharishi announces the theme of the coming year—some major goal or big project or revolutionary discovery that everybody in the Movement will focus on for the next twelve months.

Every year going back to 1957 has a slogan that describes its theme. For instance, 1970 was Maharishi's Year of Scientific Research. The yearly slogans are a handy tool for tracking Movement history.

In general, the slogans get longer and more grandiose as the decades pass. Nineteen hundred sixty-eight was Maharishi's Year of Students. Nineteen hundred seventy-eight—the year I left the Movement—was Maharishi's Year of Invincibility to Every Nation. By 1994, we'd arrived at Maharishi's Year of Global Administration Through Natural Law.

Another trend is that the early slogans are pretty down to earth while the later ones become increasingly fanciful. For instance, in 1961, Maharishi's Year of Teacher Training, the guru did actually train a bunch of TM teachers. By contrast, 2006 is Maharishi's Year of Reconstruction of the Whole World to Be Heaven on Earth. His plan to create Heaven on Earth involves developing five billion acres of land (about one seventh of the earth's land surface area) at a cost of $10 trillion.

There are other useful ways to track the Movement's evolution. A good one is to browse the ever-expanding catalog of products and services.

The basic product has always been TM instruction, and for a long time that was the only thing the Movement offered. TM was a huge fad that peaked in the mid-seventies, declined later in the decade, and then largely disappeared from the public eye.

Maharishi's first new offering in two decades was Yogic Flying, formally known as the TM-Sidhi Program and informally as "the sidhis." The Sanskrit word *sidhi* refers to the paranormal abilities of Indian legend. Flying is the best known of the yogic powers, but people who take the TM-Sidhi Program learn a bunch of them, including the power to become invisible, the ability to walk through solid walls, the ability to find lost objects, and the "strength of an elephant."

If Maharishi expected another hit, he was disappointed. It was one thing to convince John and Jane Q. Public that they could lower their blood pressure with a mantra. Convincing them that they could fly under their own power was . . . well, from a PR standpoint, the sidhis were a disaster.

In the eighties, Maharishi entered the booming market for alternative health care. His company, Maharishi Ayurveda Products International, offers everything from herbal toothpaste to "mind/body beverages" with names like Smooth Cycle and Golden Transition.

If you're in the market for a home or office complex, the Maharishi Global Construction Company will build you one. It will face true east and the roof will have the same onion-dome ornaments that top every other Maharishi building.

A Movement company called Jyotish Gems Incorporated will sell you the rubies and emeralds that your Movement astrologer prescribed to ward off the bad planets in your horoscope.

Maharishi recently came out with his own line of organic produce. There's a Web site where you can order a jar of Maharishi Organic Honey. When you click the "Order Now" button, you hear a chorus of female voices singing "Pay your money/for Maharishi honey."

Then there are the schools, colleges, and universities. Maharishi International University, Maharishi University of Management, Maharishi European Research University, Maharishi Open University, Maharishi

Spiritual University, Maharishi College of Vedic Medicine, Maharishi School of the Age of Enlightenment, and the Ideal Girls School, among others.

To finance Reconstruction of the Whole World to Be Heaven on Earth, the Movement is offering World Peace Bonds to investors. The minimum investment is $60,000 and, according to their Web site, "Bonds yield 10–15% per annum."

The Movement has a program, product, or service for every conceivable aspect of human life. Hardcore Movement types try to do all of it, which is extremely difficult. It can take up every waking moment of your life and it is very, very expensive.

When I was initiated in 1973, the basic TM course cost $75. There was a student rate of $35, which I qualified for since Todd and I were nominally studying video production technology in tech school. It was still a lot of money.

"That's two lids of really good shit!" Todd reminded me.

I have no contemporary experience in the matter, of course, but my sources tell me that a lid of really good shit goes for around $125 nowadays. That's about eight times what it cost thirty years ago.

By contrast, the TM course that I paid $35 for will now set you back $2,500. That's seventy-one times what it cost thirty years ago. And they dropped the student discount.

I wanted enlightenment, but I didn't have $35, so I had to borrow it from my long-suffering mother. Perhaps she cultivated a secret fantasy that Transcendental Meditation would do her wayward son some good.

I brought my mom's check for $35 to a farmhouse on the edge of Green Bay. I carried a brown paper bag with the rest of the prescribed offering—a bunch of freshly cut flowers, a piece of fresh fruit, and a new, clean handkerchief.

Bob greeted me at the door, invited me in, and took my check. I sat down in a beanbag chair and watched him arrange the offerings left by previous initiates. Daisies and mums and gardenias covered every flat surface in the room.

A soft voice spoke behind me.

"Hello, Geoff."

I got up and turned to see Harry wearing the same suit—a slightly baggy attempt at conservatism—he'd had on during the lecture. As I reached out to shake his hand, he placed his palms together, bowed his head a bit, and said, "Jai Guru Dev." I figured it was a special kind of greeting for enlightened people, so I did my best to mimic it. I learned later that the palm-pressing is a traditional Indian gesture of respect and the words ("hail to the divine master") a reference to Maharishi's own guru.

Harry led me into a small, tidy bedroom. Muted sunlight came through a curtained window. He closed the door and took my fruit, flowers, and handkerchief and placed them on an impromptu altar—a white cloth draped over a chest of drawers. The altar had candles and incense and several small brass bowls. The central feature was a framed photograph—or was it a painting?—of a bearded man in an orange robe. It was Maharishi's beloved guru Brahmananda Saraswati, Guru Dev himself.

Harry motioned me to stand beside him facing the altar. He lit the candles and incense and began chanting a long, slow song in Sanskrit. He sang and picked up the candles and held them before the picture of Guru Dev. He dropped a few grains of rice into a brass receptacle of water. He pressed his palms together again. I enjoyed the mysterious ritual, which seemed oddly familiar, as if I'd seen it before but forgotten it.

When the song was over, Harry fell to his knees and bowed before the altar. As he sank, he held out his hand before me, palm down, and brought it to the floor. I understood the meaning and got down on my knees and waited. The room was totally silent.

After a few moments with his head bowed, Harry rose and motioned me into one of the two chairs that faced the altar.

"Close the eyes," Harry told me.

In a barely audible voice, he told me how to meditate. He spoke my mantra, a long syllable that sounded like a note on a sitar. Then he told me he would leave the room while I had my first experience of Transcendental Meditation.

My mantra trickled through my mind like a gentle rain. Gradually, my other thoughts—hunger, bits of songs, ideas, sex fantasies—faded out as the mantra rose and fell within me. My heartbeat slowed and my breath grew faint. The mantra stretched out into a long drone and then diminished and vanished, leaving me with no mental activity other than sensations of delight in every corner of my being. This is what Maharishi calls "pure consciousness."

"Meditation is like dipping a white cloth into a bowl of colored dye," I would hear Bob explain in a lecture the next evening. "Pure consciousness is like the dye. Every time you meditate you dip the cloth in and take it out again and again and every time it gets more of the color." That is, every time you meditate you soak up more of the pure consciousness that's the source of your being and all life. You "evolve," as Maharishi says. Your life becomes more joyful and fulfilling until, eventually, you achieve a state of harmony with the universe. Enlightenment. Cosmic Consciousness.

Eventually I heard the door open and close and a body sit on the chair beside me.

"Jai Guru Dev," Harry whispered. I dismissed the mantra and sat quietly with my eyes closed for a few minutes as my mind and body returned to the world. Then I opened my eyes and saw the green, lumpy fabric of my chair.

"Jai Guru Dev," Harry said again. "It was easy?"

"Yes," I said, smiling. It was easy. I understood.

Harry instructed me to meditate twice a day, morning and evening, for twenty minutes at a stretch. I have done so every day without fail for over three decades.

I left the house and walked out into a bright summer afternoon. The sky was clear and blue. From then on, I would notice things like the color of the sky more often than I had before.

During the follow-up lectures, I heard Bob repeat a number of things that Maharishi said about TM.

"TM makes you feel more like yourself."

"Starting TM is like getting out of prison."

"Before you start TM, you look at the world through a very narrow lens. The longer you meditate, the wider and wider your lens becomes."

Earlier in the week, these slogans wouldn't have meant much to me. But after three days of meditating, I really did feel more like myself. More at home, more comfortable.

Maharishi was right, I thought. Maybe the world really would be a better place if everybody did TM.

For one of the Elect, Doug Bishop sure cussed a lot.

"Fucking old paradigm mentality!" he growled as we walked out of Wally's Big and Tall and continued our march down the main drag in Oshkosh, the Movement's latest recruiting ground.

We stopped in front of an appliance store and Doug pointed to a poster in the window with a pair of muscle-bound professional wrestlers in leotards. We walked in and headed straight for the back, where we found the store manager, a stern-looking man in a black suit, standing between two enormous refrigerators.

Doug introduced himself and explained our purpose. When the manager heard the words "Transcendental Meditation," he began to fidget.

"I'm sorry," he said. "It's store policy that we don't allow advertising."

Doug pointed at the wrestling poster and the manager scowled at us.

"Goddamn low awareness bozo!" Doug said as we left the store. He was more colorful than the average TM initiator, but it was the typical Movement complaint. Instead of griping about the manager's rude behavior or dishonesty or unfairness, he focused on the guy's state of consciousness.

I was just getting to know Doug. He looked for all the world like a standard-issue TM instructor, until you examined him a little closer and noticed that his tie was a couple of shades too loud and his hair violated the regulations by a centimeter or so.

We struck out at Schultz's Market and the hardware store next door, but the bartender at Toby's Tap said "What the hey?" and we taped a poster of Maharishi in the window next to a neon Schlitz beer sign.

By the end of the afternoon, we'd placed posters in about a quarter of the stores we'd hit. We got in Doug's old Chevy and drove back to Green Bay for the regular TM potluck supper. There would be vegetarian food, non-alcoholic beverages, a group meditation, and a tape of Maharishi. Afterward, Doug might haul out his guitar, or somebody might put on an album by the Movement's own softcore folk-rock group, the Natural Tendency (including songs like "Rest Is the Basis of Activity" and "Water the Root to Enjoy the Fruit").

We got to Doug's apartment just as Bob and Harry were arriving.

"There is beautiful news," said Harry with great decorum. "Maharishi has given us a beautiful new gift. A *wonderful* new university. Maharishi International University.

"Studying at MIU is the fastest evolutionary path in human history. You reach Cosmic Consciousness with your bachelor's degree. You reach God Consciousness with your master's degree and you reach Unity Consciousness with your Ph.D."

He had a supply of application forms with him. Doug and Trisha and I filled them out on the spot.

Events passed quickly now that I had a purpose in life. My application was accepted almost immediately. I convinced my mother to write a check for the tuition. I left tech school and my Green Bay apartment and said brief good-byes to the handful of non-Movement friends who were still floating around northern Wisconsin. I packed some sweatshirts and jeans, my tape player, and a few tapes of Tim Buckley and the Bonzo Dog Band.

On a frigid day in January of 1974, I got on a plane and flew to Santa Barbara, California, the site of the original MIU campus. During the taxi ride from the airport, I sat in the back seat admiring the palm trees swaying in the gentle wind and recalled Trisha's vision of MIU. Geodesic domes connected by monorails. George Harrison playing sitar by the pool.

The taxi let me off at a Spanish-style apartment complex with the blue and gold logo of Maharishi International University on a sign out front. Looking back, I realize that I'd flown halfway across the continent with no clue about the place I'd be living, which was how we did things back in those heady days. If Trisha was disappointed by the drab concrete and lack of monorails, she didn't let on. In any case, we all understood that the concrete walls were just the material world, just temporary.

By the end of the first day, I'd made a dozen new friends. On the morning of the second day, there was a general meeting in the main lecture hall. I've never seen a crowd that was so turned-on, so full of smiles and alert eyes.

Up at the podium, a fair-haired man with a boyish face approached the microphone: Dr. Robert Keith Wallace, the founding President of Maharishi International University. He beamed at the crowd.

"Is everybody having a good time?" he asked. The room exploded with laughter and applause.

I always get suspicious when people say that their spiritual technique is the only way," Sarah told me. "I got some of that from TM people."

"Oh God," I said. "That drove me totally nuts."

We were driving through Iowa City, a favorite weekend getaway in my MIU days.

"Was that part of the reason you left?" Sarah asked. "I don't think you ever told me."

"That was part of it," I said. "There were a bunch of reasons."

"You didn't like the food?"

"I actually did like the food. Ringo Starr didn't, but I did."

"You caught Maharishi fooling around with his secretary?"

I smiled. "I only saw him in person once."

I remembered sitting for hours on a hard, uncomfortable bench in the MIU fieldhouse, surrounded by thousands of people staring in rapt silence at the tiny man far away in a circle of white light framed by lavish bouquets of flowers. Along with the heat and the discomfort and the boredom, I remembered wondering what all the fuss was about.

"It's complicated," I said. "In the beginning I probably would have put up with anything because I was having such good results from TM. I felt better, I was happier. Jeez . . . it could have been Jonestown and I wouldn't have cared.

"Another thing is that MIU was kind of an island in the Movement. Maharishi was treating us like his favorite children, grooming us to be his own caste of Brahmins.

"It was actually a huge amount of fun, at least in the beginning. I remember feeling like I was part of a family with all the love and support, but with a purpose, something bigger than yourself. We were spiritual warriors and kids having a blast, all at the same time."

"It sounds a bit like Harry Potter," said Sarah. I chuckled.

"Yeah. Every kid fantasizes about leaving the boring world and escaping to Hogwarts Academy. I did it for real.

"The problem for me was that none of it went anywhere. When you start TM you notice big changes in your life, but you hit a plateau after a while. Maharishi kept saying that the Age of Enlightenment was just around the corner, but it never showed up. And the Movement changed. It was a lot looser in the beginning. You could get away with wearing blue jeans or long hair, but there was more and more pressure to look conservative."

"How come?"

"Well, I asked one of the dorm advisors about that—why we were supposed to wear suits and ties even when we were sitting around at night doing homework. He said 'You're always a representative of Maharishi. You never know when a reporter from *Time* magazine is going to come in and interview you.'"

I gave a wry giggle and Sarah smiled.

"Of course, most of the people at MIU were old hippies, and they didn't really take to a dress code. So you'd see guys wearing bright yellow jackets with green ties, but that didn't last long. When people came back from the first Yogic Flying courses, they looked like Wall Street yuppies. They were the elite, and everybody started to copy them."

"So you didn't fit in?"

"I guess I fit in early on. I wanted enlightenment as much as anybody. I wanted to be part of the next big social transformation. I really believed what Maharishi said—that you can transform society by teaching meditation to as many people as possible.

"But every year there were more and more rules, more mandatory activities. When I graduated from MIU in '78, it was easy for me to wander off and do the next thing.

"What I saw after that made me glad I left when I did. There was the constant fund-raising hype for grandiose projects that never materialized. The Movement started backing political candidates—that drove me up the wall. Now Maharishi's going on about the apocalypse like Pat Robertson."

"You're getting angry," Sarah said.

"Well, yeah. I joined the Movement in good faith. I was interested in meditation, spiritual evolution. If Maharishi had been doing the kind of stuff back then that he's doing now, I would have turned and run in the opposite direction."

We drove in silence for a while. Sarah held the convertible's steering wheel in one hand and mine in the other. I watched her short, brown hair fluttering around her face in the wind. This was my home, and I was content.

"Sometimes I look back on it and I feel cheated, betrayed," I said with a sigh. "But I guess I betrayed myself. I went into the Movement with all kinds of preconceptions about spirituality. I wanted the Movement to be some kind of counterculture utopia. I doubt that was ever what Maharishi had in mind."

We both chuckled.

"Maybe . . ." I said tentatively, "instead of asking why people leave the Movement, it makes more sense to ask why they stay. I mean, it's great when you're a kid—you're idealistic and you don't mind sleeping on a cot and living on rice and lentils. But the years go by and the sacrifices and the frustrations pile up.

"The people who stay really are a select group. I used to wonder why anybody would stick with it, but I think it's clearer now. It's because of Maharishi. They got into it because of him and they stay because of him, even though hardly anybody's seen him in person for decades. You either love him or you don't, and I didn't."

As we left Iowa City we passed the first road sign for our destination:

FAIRFIELD: 60 MILES

"Of course," I said, "now I'm going back."

Chapter 4

The Golden Dome of Pure Knowledge

The drive to Fairfield took us through long miles of prairie past herds of cows, silos, right-to-life billboards, farmhouses with many lightning rods, and the palace of Emperor Ming the Merciless.

"What is *that*?" asked Sarah, jabbing her finger at the alien layer cake with multiple peaked roofs topped by onion domes.

"I've only seen them in pictures," I told my wife, "but it's a Movement building. There's a company called Maharishi Global Construction that builds them. They all look pretty much alike, although that's gotta be one of the bigger ones."

Sarah read the sign by the parking lot:

BOOKS ARE FUN

"That's Earl Kaplan's company," I said. "He was in my class at MIU."

Earl stayed in Fairfield and went into business. His company, Books Are Fun, purchases "more books per single title than most retailers in the world"[2] and resells them from on-site displays in corporations, hospitals, schools, and other venues. In 1999, Reader's Digest bought out Earl for $300 million and made him one of Maharishi's richest followers.

That sort of thing—wealth and power—was supposed to happen to everybody in the Movement. It didn't, mostly.

"There it is," I said as we crossed the Fairfield city limits and approached my alma mater. We passed the building where Earl and I used to live, one of a string of squat dorms painted Movement gold.

"Let's turn in up here," I said, pointing at the front entrance of the campus. Sarah swung the convertible past the MAHARISHI UNIVERSITY OF MANAGEMENT sign through the old stone gate.

"I liked the original name better," said Sarah. "Why did they change it? Is it a business school now?"

"No, that's just how the Movement works. Every few years, Maharishi reorganizes everything and comes up with a bunch of new names."

As I finished my sentence, the front end of the car clunked into a huge pothole. I looked down the street and saw an obstacle course of broken pavement, as if there hadn't been any road maintenance since I left.

Sarah gingerly navigated the car around cracks and holes past the venerable quad with its hundred-year-old buildings. The campus hadn't changed much; it could still be Parsons College, the small liberal arts school that Maharishi purchased in the early seventies. Except for the huge yellow bulge where the football field used to be.

"There's the Golden Dome of Pure Knowledge," I said, nodding at the Movement's holiest of holies. The dome—which didn't exist in my day—went up when there were enough Yogic Flyers to require a separate building for group levitation.

I scanned the dome and imagined eyes inside watching as I drove through the middle of campus in a top-down convertible wearing blue jeans.

"Geoff, you're shaking like a leaf!" Sarah said.

Blue jeans! After throwing them on for twenty years without a care in the world, I'd forgotten how much Maharishi hates them. I looked around nervously, but no one was staring and pointing. In fact, the campus seemed deserted. *Calm down, calm down,* I said to myself.

We followed the main drag as it curved past the silent dining hall and lifeless student union toward the dormitories.

"Let's go see my old dorm," I said, pointing the way. We parked by the building that had been my home for two very happy years; the place where, after a month of solid meditation, I got my best taste of Cosmic Consciousness; the place where I told Beth I loved her.

The nostalgia drained out of me when I saw the peeling paint, the weeds, and the hanging baskets of dead flowers. I felt like I'd come to the wrong place. I scrambled up crumbling stairs onto the concrete deck where the gang used to lie in the afternoon sun drinking smoothies and talking about enlightenment.

"This really isn't safe," said Sarah, sidestepping a piece of rubble.

I tried the front door, but it was locked. Taped behind the clouded glass was a sign with flowery lettering inside a border of leaves and vines:

PLEASE DO NOT USE THIS SOUTHERN ENTRANCE

We left the campus and drove into town. We passed the row of Victorian mansions that date from the heyday of the railroad and seem so outsized in this modest farm community. As we approached the town square, Sarah pointed to a sign that said FAIRFIELD—10,000 PARTNERS IN PROGRESS. I told her the population hadn't changed since my day, when perhaps a tenth of the "partners" were followers of Maharishi.

The square was the same block of classic Americana I knew by heart— four streets of stores with old-fashioned false fronts facing a manicured lawn with a white gazebo in the middle for summer band concerts. My old college hangouts were still there. Torino's Pizza and the Co-Ed movie theater could have been preserved in formaldehyde.

The gazebo reminded me of an evening, not long after MIU moved to town, when I discovered what Fairfield kids do for fun.

"Doug and I went to the Co-Ed to see *The Devil's Rain* with Ernest Borgnine," I said. "It got out around eleven p.m. and we didn't want to go back to campus, so we hung out in the gazebo. Fairfield is usually dead as a doorknob in the evening, but the square was packed with cars bumper to bumper. Every high school kid in town was out cruising. The weird thing was that they weren't going anywhere. All these Mustangs and Barracudas were driving around the square in circles over and over at about ten miles an hour. When a kid got to a stop sign, he'd sit there for a while and rev his engine, then he'd turn right and drive to the next stop sign and rev his engine again. They were still doing it when we left around midnight. Doug said they were trying to attain escape velocity."

As Sarah rounded the square, I noticed that the crowd on the sidewalk hadn't changed. The same elderly farmers in dungarees coming out of the hardware store, the same portly businessmen going into the bank. It probably wasn't much different a hundred years ago.

"Let's get something to eat," said Sarah, who'd driven the whole five hours from our home in Wisconsin. We pulled into the parking lot of the HyVee grocery, the store that Doug and I used to rely on when we wanted something other than brown rice. Sarah turned off the engine while I stared at the vanity license plate on the vehicle in front of us.

It said ANANDA, Sanskrit for bliss.

Inside the store, Sarah and I headed for the deli section in search of potato salad and deviled eggs, our traditional road food. We walked through the aisles past the sort of groceries I remembered from the old days—canned ham, Fritos—alongside incongruous items like "calming tea" and jars of clarified butter from the Exceedingly Fine Ghee Company.

"Look around at the people," I said softly, "and try to match them with the food."

It was a pretty easy game. The ruddy-faced gent in overalls would go for the ham and the Indian matron in the bright orange sari would choose the textured vegetable protein.

Our motel room was standard-issue Best Western, a big improvement from the old days of the railroad hotel. Sarah sat cross-legged on the bed reading her mystery novel over a plate of deviled eggs as I flipped through the Fairfield telephone directory. Every page amplified the culture shock.

"Look at all these Indian names," I said to Sarah. "Krisnamurthy, Rajeesh, Agarwal. I lived here for five years in the seventies and the whole town was as lily white as it could be. And get a load of these businesses: Bio-Energetic Wellness, Amrita Aroma Therapy, Time Portal Publications."

When I lived there, Fairfield businesses had names like Dotty's Sewing Nook and Acme Sandblasting. If a place called Amrita Aroma Therapy had the nerve to show its face on the square, it would have been run out of town by the local chapter of the John Birch Society.

"What on earth happened here?" I said, taking the deviled egg Sarah offered me.

W e drove to campus early after breakfast the next day. Although there was nobody around to notice, we were dressed in Movement-grade clothing—a jacket and tie for me and a long dress for Sarah. There would be no repeat of the previous day's denim fiasco.

"Now *this* is what a college should look like." I told Sarah as we walked across the old quad of my alma mater, admiring the classic buildings of red brick and dust-colored stone. Since we both grew up in university families, the ivy-covered walls made us feel at home.

The buildings on the old quad go back to the late 1800s and the founding of Parsons College, a tiny Presbyterian liberal arts school on the edge of Fairfield. Parsons went bankrupt in the early seventies, around the time that Maharishi International University was getting too big for its original home in the Santa Barbara apartment complex. Maharishi went campus shopping and acquired Parsons at a bargain rate.

"That's the chapel where I had my graduation ceremony," I said. We walked up to the front entrance where I'd posed for a group photo with the forty-odd members of MIU's third graduating class. The sturdy wooden door was faded and peeling and locked.

Sarah and I strolled along the old stones of the chapel's cloister walk. It was still early—around eight a.m.—and the only sounds came from starlings and the wind.

"This is where the administration offices used to be," I said as we approached an ivied building with a sagging roof. "The President, the Vice President." I looked through a cloudy window at a hallway with piles of cardboard boxes and chairs stacked on tables.

We walked around the quad to the building where I came for my housing assignment on the morning I arrived at the new MIU campus. It looked deserted. The door was locked, but there was a sign:

PLEASE DO NOT USE THIS SOUTHERN ENTRANCE

"What do they have against southern entrances?" Sarah asked. I shrugged.

We left the old quad and crossed Dr. Robert Keith Wallace Drive, named after the founding president of MIU. The street that bore his name separated the old part of campus with its Victorian buildings from the much-larger part that went up in the 1960s.

"Parsons College nearly went under in the late fifties," I told Sarah. "Their enrollment was shrinking to nothing and they were desperate for new students.

"In 1959 they hired a new president—a guy named Millard Roberts—whose job was to save the school at any cost. He came up with a plan called the Parsons Idea, which was basically to accept students who couldn't get in to any other college in the United States.

"It worked pretty well at first, but it really took off with the Vietnam War."

"Ah," said Sarah. "The student deferment?"

"Yeah," I replied. "For a lot of guys, Parsons was the last hope for getting a deferment and avoiding the draft. Enrollment went from the hundreds into the thousands practically overnight. The old Parsons campus was way too small to handle all the new students, so they built this."

I made a gesture that encompassed a hundred acres of the ugliest brick and concrete facilities this side of cold war Romania.

"It only lasted a few years, though. The government got rid of most student deferments in 1971. And Parsons had lowered its academic standards so far by then that it lost its accreditation. It closed down in 1973. Then Maharishi bought it."

I recalled the brief town/gown honeymoon during MIU's first year in Iowa. It started a few days before the first chartered buses arrived from the original MIU location in Santa Barbara.

A work party of townies, led by the mayor of Fairfield, came out to campus with lawnmowers and rakes and hedge trimmers to clean up the place. Local business owners put up WELCOME MIU signs in their store windows. There was a big barbecue with chicken for the townies and vegetarian pizza for the meditators and smiles and speeches all around.

And that was that. The meditators retreated into their rooms and shut their doors and the locals went back to their farms and churches. Within months, Fairfield was as segregated as the old South.

Like most Movement people, I was too busy developing higher states of consciousness to notice the growing rift between town and gown. I got a clue in the spring of 1977, my junior year, when I went jogging with my friend Jamie.

We were running down a dirt road about a mile out of town. As we passed an isolated farmhouse, I heard a door open and slam shut. I turned to see a little kid—he might have been eight or nine—charging toward us with his fists clenched and his face screwed up in a grimace.

"Fucking goddamn gurus! Fucking goddamn gurus!" he yelled. He stopped by the side of the road, picked up a rock, and hurled it at us.

My daydream ended when Sarah poked me in the arm. "Look over there," she said, pointing at the Golden Dome of Pure Knowledge and the crowd of men pouring out of it into the morning sun. Another crowd, all women, emerged from an identical dome at the opposite end of the field that used to be the home turf of the Parsons Wildcats.

We watched the crowds spill out of the domes—lean, balding men in pale suits and serious-looking women. In spite of our camouflage clothing, I felt dreadfully conspicuous. Sarah squeezed my hand and I realized that I was on the verge of hyperventilating for the second time in twenty-four hours.

What is wrong? I wondered. I lived in this place for five years and it never made me gasp for breath before. Fortunately, nobody turned to stare. The one person who noticed us—a middle-aged woman in a floral dress—gave a friendly smile and walked on. My heart rate sank down toward normal.

As we continued down Wallace Drive, I noticed that many of the old buildings had acquired new names. The main classroom building, known as the Learning Center in my day, bore a sign identifying it as Yagyavalkya Hall. My Sanskrit wasn't up to that one, although I was able to figure out that Annapurna, the new name for the cafeteria, meant filled with food.

The Student Union remained the Student Union. We walked down a dim hallway past the entrance to the Union Theatre where I saw Andy Kaufman do his Elvis impersonation, an act he'd honed on TM courses before he became famous.

The hall was empty except for an old cork board that was missing most of its cork.

"Did I tell you the story about the money on the bulletin board?" I asked Sarah. She shook her head. "I used to check this board every day. People would post all kinds of ads and announcements and stuff. One day I saw a ten-dollar bill pinned to a note that said 'I found this on the stairs.' The money stayed up there for the better part of a week. Somebody finally took it, and I'd be really surprised if it wasn't the person who lost the money."

Sarah smiled. She likes that kind of story.

The hall took us past the old snack bar. The door was locked, but I could see the linoleum-covered table in the corner where Doug held court in his scarves and fedora telling slightly off-color stories, a sort of herbal tea Truman Capote. I could see Beth standing in the crowd laughing in delight, always in the middle of whatever was going on, always one of the guys.

We walked into the Union's main lobby and sat on a couch next to a large picture window with a view of the old Parsons College field house.

"That's where Maharishi was lecturing the one time I saw him in person," I told Sarah.

Good lord, I thought, I know every inch of this place like it was my body. It's the old comfortable, familiar space, but . . . what did they do to the walls?

A huge mural covered the length and breadth of the Union lobby. Exotic and faintly Oriental, it showed a formal garden on a great estate with fountains, ornamental trees, manicured shrubbery, and peacocks parading down a stately white road.

Given the context, I knew that the mural wasn't just random decoration. It was a lesson, an official policy statement. It was Maharishi saying "This is what all landscapes should look like and what they will look like in the Age of Enlightenment."

I considered an ornamental shrub in the mural's foreground, carved by topiary artists into a column of globes. There was no stem—the spheres of greenery were hovering suspended in the air, one above the other. In the Age of Enlightenment, even the shrubbery will levitate.

When we left the Student Union and stepped onto Wallace Drive, I looked at the cracked pavement and weedy lawns and compared them to the otherworldly perfection of the garden in the mural. Maharishi has a long way to go.

The Dreier Building stood out among the nineteenth-century classics on the old campus like a gong in a string quartet. It was much smaller than Books Are Fun, but it had the same compulsive symmetry and little onion domes.

Sarah and I walked through the stately front door into a lobby furnished with wall-to-wall shoe racks. A couple of children in school uniforms sat on a nearby bench untying their sneakers. They carried their shoes to the shelves and placed them neatly amid dozens of pairs of Nikes, sandals, Reeboks, boots, wingtips, and at least one pair of vintage Earth Shoes. Their footgear stowed, the children padded off in their stocking feet.

"This is new," I whispered to Sarah, pulling her to the bench. We sat down and removed our shoes and carried them to the rack. I stared at the crowded shelves and wondered how on earth I was supposed to find mine again. I picked an empty slot as close to the front door as possible.

Third shelf up, two over . . . third shelf up, two over. I knew I'd forget it by the time we left. I thought of the sidhis, the yogic powers. Wasn't there a sidhi for finding lost objects? That must be how they did it.

We walked out of the lobby into a large, sunny atrium. As atriums go, it could pass in a Wisconsin law office or accounting firm except for the dozens of gold and pastel posters with a little picture of Maharishi in the corner. Sarah was deeply engrossed in one of them. I joined her and read the following proclamation:

PEOPLE DO NOT KNOW THAT MANY MISFORTUNES AND EVEN DISEASES ARISE FROM LACK OF PROPER ORIENTATION OF THE HOUSES IN WHICH THEY LIVE AND WORK.

"Geoff? Geoff . . . Gilpin?"

The voice was chipper and full of amusement. Before I turned, I knew the rough face I'd see.

"Ron?"

He'd lost a lot of weight, and he wasn't wearing his signature three-piece green suit with the cowboy belt, but it was definitely Ron Edgars, my neighbor in the dorm we called Good Old 109.

"Ron! Wow, it's . . ." He had me in a bear hug before I could finish. In spite of his now-trim figure, he was still a big and commanding guy. He stepped back and gave me a penetrating look.

"I didn't think you were gonna come back," he said.

"Oh . . . well, Sarah and I . . . this is my wife, Sarah . . . we were in Iowa." (God, that was lame.)

Ron and Sarah shook hands and he gave her the same probing look I'd received. I briefly wondered if he was practicing the sidhi for reading minds, then I told myself to cut it out.

After some pleasantries about where we lived and how we were doing, Ron invited us to join him in his office on the second floor. The trip turned into an impromptu tour of the new building.

"They finished it a couple of months ago," he said. "It was supposed to be for the new computer science department, but as soon as it was done, Maharishi said 'Get everybody in there now!' He's really strong on the architecture these days.

"The front door has to face east," Ron said. "You really don't want another door, but you can't tell that to the fire department, so we have an exit on the north side. That's the next best after east."

We climbed a staircase to the second floor and Ron walked over to a railing at the edge of the mezzanine. He pointed over the railing into empty space. "This is the *brahamastan*," he said. That was a new one on me, but I took it to be Sanskrit for atrium.

"It's big. It goes up from the ground floor to the *kalash* at the top." He pointed upward and I craned my neck to follow. There was a skylight in the peak of the roof crowned by one of the onion-domed ornaments. "The kalash brings in the *devas*," Ron said.

Devas—angels, gods, spirits. It was starting to make sense.

"The devas come down and hang out in the brahamastan," he continued. He went on to describe the benefits of living and working in a building designed according to the principles of Maharishi Architecture—better health, more creativity—but I was zoning out. I looked up at the sunlit kalash. A rain of golden particles, tumbling and sparkling in the sunshine, drifted down and filled the atrium. Dust, not angels.

"You're not supposed to walk through the brahamastan," said Ron, pointing down at the ground floor. "It's just for the devas. Lots of room just for the devas."

I thought I heard a bit of disapproval in his voice, as if he resented allocating so much of the floor plan to invisible beings. I remembered Ron as one of the most worldly, down-to-earth people in the Movement. He toed the party line in word and deed, as most did, but you were never quite sure how much of it he believed. It was hard to imagine the old Ron going along with this strange architectural stuff.

We proceeded along the mezzanine to the office where Ron worked as a university fund-raiser. His desk and computer occupied one corner of a cramped room he shared with several coworkers. I began to understand his resentment of the devas.

"You're about the last one to show up," Ron said as he settled into his chair. "People come and go . . . it's like a revolving door here. You stayed away a lot longer than most."

"Have you seen Beth?" I asked. Ron sighed and pursed his lips. Back in the day, he was one of several guys at MIU who carried a torch for Beth Adair.

"Oh, Beth, Beth," Ron said wistfully. "She was living in town, but I haven't seen her for at least a year."

Since we were moving on to old home week, Sarah excused herself and left for the motel to get some work done. I sat down next to Ron's desk and we reminisced as a steady stream of his coworkers came and went around us.

"You left in, what, '78?" he asked, and I nodded. "So you're probably not a sidha." I shook my head. "You're missing out," he said in a slightly scolding tone. "Yogic Flying is the greatest. You shoulda been here for the Taste of Utopia course in '83. Seven thousand sidhas flying together in the dome! Man! The experiences!"

I smiled and did my best to look impressed by thousands of people hopping on foam rubber. "So, have you been here the whole time?" I asked.

"Mostly," he said. "I left in '85 and went back to Ohio. I got an MBA and worked for the state. I tried it . . . I did it. But, ya know, it's all mud out there.

"I came back and settled down. That's one big change—a lot of us grew up and got married and had kids. And it's more fragmented than it was. It used to be that everybody lived on campus. It was pretty isolated in the beginning, but in the eighties a lot of people moved into town and started having normal lives—families, jobs, houses. The ones who still live on campus are mostly your true-blue roos."

"Uh, 'roos?'"

Ron laughed. "You never heard that? The townies came up with it. They started out calling us gurus as a swear word and then it got shortened to just roos. That's what a lot of us call ourselves now, but it's way too undignified for some people."

I must have had a puzzled expression on my face. Ron gave me a broad grin.

"You see," he continued in the tone of a professor expounding on a favorite topic, "the Movement in Fairfield isn't anywhere near as homogenized as it used to be. You've got the whole spectrum. Some people have gone off the program totally. Some come in for the domes, but that's the only contact they have. Some people try to stay pure and keep up with the knowledge as best they can and still have a life. Then you've got your *reeeal* hardcore types."

"You mean . . . like bliss ninnies?"

"Ohhhh, more like your brainwashed zombies." The way he said it— cheerfully with a wry smile—reminded me of why I liked him.

"So where do you fit in?" I asked.

"Me? I'm just a family guy. I raise my kids, do my job here, get some laughs now and then. I tried different things, but I always come back to Maharishi. Nobody else thinks as big as he does. I probably wouldn't be alive if it wasn't for him."

Ron started shuffling papers and talking about getting to work, but I had to ask him about the warning signs I'd seen on southern entrances.

"That's the most important rule in Vedic architecture," he said.

I dimly recalled hearing Maharishi speak of India's Vedic period— circa 1,500 B.C.—as a golden age. A time of peace and plenty when everybody lived according to the rules of the Vedas, the ancient sacred texts.

"Of all the directions, south is the worst," Ron said. He pulled a brochure out of his desk and showed me one of its gold and pastel pages.

AUSPICIOUS AND INAUSPICIOUS INFLUENCES

DUE TO ORIENTATION OF BUILDINGS.

There was a picture of a house surrounded by arrows coming from the eight points of the compass. Each direction had a label:

INAUSPICIOUS ENTRANCE FACING WEST:

INFLUENCE OF POVERTY.

INAUSPICIOUS ENTRANCE FACING SOUTHWEST:

INFLUENCE OF QUARRELING.

INAUSPICIOUS ENTRANCE FACING NORTHWEST:

INFLUENCE OF MENTAL INSTABILITY.

And so on. South was worst, with "All Negative Influences, Problems and Suffering." North is okay ("Happiness") and east is best ("Enlightenment, Affluence, Fulfillment").

"That's the basic idea," said Ron. "Invite the good guys in and keep out the bad guys."

I chuckled and raised my eyebrows. "It sounds like I've got a lot of catching up to do," I said.

"Don't worry," Ron replied with a jovial grin. "You stick around a couple weeks and it'll be like you never left."

We shook hands and agreed to meet for lunch at noon.

On the way out of the building, I stopped in the atrium, smiled into the warm sunshine pouring down on me from the skylight, and tried to remember what Ron said about the brahamastan.

Oh jeez . . . I'm standing in the angels! I scurried over to the wall and looked around furtively.

"This is going too far," I thought. I don't believe in angels, at least not the Maharishi kind that demands a particular style of architecture and then squats in the middle of it. But I was acting like I believed it. When in Rome, maybe.

I left the atrium, sticking as close to the wall as possible, and walked into the lobby to retrieve my shoes. I stared at the dozens of pairs arranged neatly side-by-side on shelf after shelf and tried to recall the little formula I had for locating my own. Sure enough, it was gone. I would have to examine every shoe in the lobby, which I did, beginning with the pair of ladies' sensible flats in the upper left corner.

I was about halfway down when it hit me.

"Bad guys?"

Sarah—who is more of an explorer than her husband—decided to visit the Fairfield town square before returning to the motel. She parked the convertible across from the Co-Ed Theatre and was pleased when the parking meter gave her an hour for one dime.

The gazebo in the town square made her smile, as did the nineteenth-century false fronts on the old buildings. There were the businesses you'd expect for a rural Iowa town—the hardware store, the auto supply shop, the Radio Shack—but also a storefront Tarot reader.

As she walked around the square, Sarah counted two Indian restaurants, two Thai restaurants, two Chinese, and one Italian—a 700 percent increase in ethnic dining opportunities since my day.

She stopped into a clothing store called Natural Selections. Every item in the store was made from 100 percent natural fibers—cotton, wool, hemp. Most of the garments were tan or off-white, but there were also muted earth tones.

Sarah left the store and walked into a nearby dress shop. The clerk was a matronly woman clad in shiny blue polyester. Chrome shelves and mannequins displayed boxy dresses made from slick synthetic fabrics, some decorated with sequins or rhinestones. Sarah left quickly.

The next stop was the one-store downtown that identified itself as a Movement operation. The window of the Health and Wholeness boutique had a sign advertising Maharishi Ayurvedic Products. Sarah walked in and looked around at the displays of books, creams, teas, pills, fragrances, and compact discs, most of which carried Maharishi's picture.

Sarah was thumbing through a rack of CDs when the store clerk, an attractive young woman with short blond hair, came over and smiled.

"Can I help you find something?" she asked in a friendly voice.

"I was thinking I'd enjoy some traditional Indian music," Sarah said.

The clerk flipped through CDs, picked one out, and handed it to Sarah. "This guy's excellent. He's the lead flute player for the National Orchestra of India." She picked out another one. "I like this sitar player a lot . . . this one's one of our best sellers. When will you be listening to it?"

"Oh . . . pretty much any time."

"Well, you can listen to *this* one at any time," the clerk said, handing Sarah another CD. The label read:

MAHARISHI GANDHARVA VEDA
THE ETERNAL MUSIC OF NATURE
MELODY FOR INCREASED ENERGY AND BLISS

Sure enough, the label said "Can be played at any time."

"How do you plan to use it?" the clerk asked.

Sarah cocked her head slightly. No sales clerk had ever asked about her plans for a compact disc before.

"Well . . . I'll probably use it as background music. Maybe when I'm driving or at home reading or doing housework."

"Oh, no, you wouldn't want to do that," the clerk said, without a blip in her friendly and matter-of-fact manner. "That would divide the attention.

"I guess if you really want to have it on while you do other things, you could put it on in another room and shut the door so that you couldn't hear it and it wouldn't divide your attention." The clerk smiled and brightened. "You could even set the CD player to repeat play and keep it going twenty-four hours a day. As long as you couldn't hear it."

Sarah bought the CD, took it back to the car, tore off the cellophane wrapper, and put it into the car's CD player and turned up the volume just to be contrary.

At noon sharp, I arrived at Annapurna Hall and found the main entrance locked. The door that I'd opened thousands of times en route to breakfast, lunch, and dinner was inauspiciously pointed south, the direction of "all negative influences."

I followed a group of men in cream-colored suits around the building to its new entrance. By that time, I was getting pretty savvy with directions, and I was very surprised to see that the new door to the dining hall faced west—the direction of poverty!

One of the suit guys smiled and held the door open for me, and I walked into a cloud of familiar smells. I stood in the lobby waiting for Ron and watching the door open and close over and over.

"How's it supposed to work?" I wondered. Is the inauspicious entrance letting in poverty each time somebody opens the door? And why would they shut down one bad door just to open another? I suppose I'd rather have a western entrance letting in poverty than a northwestern entrance for "mental instability."

By a few minutes after twelve, the lobby had a good-sized crowd. There were a fair number of young adults—teenagers and twenty-somethings in ties and dresses and conservative haircuts. There were just as many, if not more, middle-aged people with gray or thinning hair, glasses, and the odd paunch or stoop.

Ron came in, accompanied by a very lovely woman.

"Hey!" he said with a big smile when he saw me. "You remember Sheila Hardesty?" I didn't at first.

"I think you knew my ex-husband, Frank," she explained. Then it came back. Frank lived next door to me in Good Old 109 and Sheila lived on the other side of the building in the "ladies' wing." The place was an alchemical furnace of romance. Along with many brief and extended flings, Old 109 produced two marriages in my senior year. Neither lasted.

"I remember coming to visit Frank," Sheila said to me, "and stopping to read the poetry on your door. There was the one about radioactive marmalade pancakes."

"I'd forgotten about that," I said.

Ron led us into the cafeteria. It hadn't changed a bit in twenty-five years—the same steam tables held the same stir-fried vegetables, rice, and tofu scrambled with turmeric and ghee. The industrial juice-squeezer was in its familiar corner, flanked by barrels of citrus fruit. We filled up trays of food and found a table in the dining room.

I was about to pick up my fork when Ron and Sheila bowed their heads in silence. People at tables around us were doing the same, and I quickly joined in. When I opened my eyes, I noticed that quite a few people kept theirs closed for a very long grace.

"Have you been in the domes yet?" Sheila asked cheerfully, tucking into her scrambled tofu. I sheepishly admitted that I did plain old TM and not Yogic Flying.

"You'll love the domes," she said. "Maharishi calls them 'the washing machines of the world.' You really should get the sidhis. Ron said you're a writer, right? Flying is the best for creativity."

Sheila told me about her job in the university's PR department. Like Ron, she seemed professional and down-to-earth, the sort of person who could easily get a job at a regular university. She and her second husband had a daughter enrolled in the Maharishi School of the Age of Enlightenment.

We ate bok choy in silence as I looked around the dining room. The ceiling was cracked and peeling, but the place felt lived-in and comfortable. The younger types were smiling and laughing. The middle-aged contingent in their off-white suits and dresses were eating quietly or having friendly conversations. The food was good, too.

"It's an older crowd than I remember," I said.

"Uh-huh," said Ron. "Most of the people left in the Movement are in their forties or fifties. The counterculture grown up. Not a lot of new people. I always wondered why we were the ones who got to experience all this. Why was it our generation?"

As I took a sip of peach nectar, I noticed one guy sitting by himself at a table in the corner who had been saying grace with his eyes closed for about ten minutes.

Sheila asked me what I wanted to do on my visit, and I told her I was hoping to watch the Maharishi Channel.

"We have that," she said. "Why don't you come over after dinner?"

Around 7:30 that evening, I walked down the row of old Parsons fraternity houses to the building where Sheila and her family lived. Like all the other frats, this one faced the direction of "all negative influences." I entered through a side door ("lack of creativity" and "lack of vitality") that led to a dark corridor crammed with bicycles, snow gear, boxes, and wires hanging from the ceiling. I expected the large common area I remembered, but the building had been completely remodeled—the interior with the old dorm rooms gutted and rebuilt as apartments.

I followed the dim, stuffy corridor as it snaked around past apartment doorways and shoe racks until I came to a dead end. A door opened and a tall, gaunt man in a cream-colored suit emerged. He was bending down to pick up his shoes when he saw me.

"Hi," I said. He glared at me. "Can you tell me how to get to the Hardestys?"

He pointed at a door and then stomped off in the direction of all negative influences.

The door led to a stairway illuminated by a bare light bulb. I found Sheila's place at the top. I sat down on a chair by the shoe rack, removed my sneakers, and put them on the shelf next to a pair of little pink boots. Sheila opened the door when I knocked.

"Hi, Geoff, come on in." Unlike the dingy hall, the Hardesty's apartment was tidy, open, and airy with a lot of natural wood. "Would you like tea?" Sheila asked. We walked into the kitchen and she pointed to a shelf with boxes of herbal teas, each with a little picture of Maharishi. There was "cooling" tea, "warming" tea, "calming," "invigorating," and "be trim." Sheila selected the cooling tea for me, "because you've been traveling."

"My husband has to work this evening, and I'm afraid that I have to run," she said, handing me my cup of cooling tea, "but you're welcome to stay and watch TV."

A bedroom door opened and a little girl of maybe four or five ran in to the room. She was wearing the green checkerboard dress that I'd seen earlier at the Maharishi School on campus.

"Lakshmi, this is Geoff," said Sheila to her daughter. "He's one of mommy's old friends." Lakshmi gave me a shy smile.

"Geoff was one of the first Movement people in Fairfield, even before mommy and daddy came," said Sheila. The little girl stared at me with big eyes as if her mother had introduced a thawed-out Neanderthal.

We walked into the living room and Sheila picked up the remote that controlled the satellite receiver and clicked on the Maharishi Channel.

"I have to take Lakshmi to her class," Sheila said as she helped her daughter with her jacket. "Make yourself at home."

I thanked her and said good-bye as they walked out. On a hunch, I got up and opened the door. It wasn't locked. That was common enough in my day—hardly anybody at MIU locked their door back then—but I was surprised that the custom continued, surprised and pleased that some of the old trusting community spirit survived.

I settled in on the living room sofa in front of the TV. The program was a cartoon of some kind. An Indian goddess—I recognized her as the other Lakshmi, she of wealth and good fortune—stood in a lotus as a computer-generated shower of gold coins gently rained down on her. She smiled and raised her arms as the coins piled up at her feet to the sound of cheerful flute music. She raised and lowered her arms. The coins fell, twirling and shining. The golden piles grew until they reached Lakshmi's waist, at which point they drained away and the process started again. The animation looped around, over and over. Coins falling and falling. Lakshmi raising and lowering her arms. The flute. The coins. Over and over.

Chapter 5

The Jerusalem Experiment

J amie was the first guy at MIU with a pair of running shoes, blue Pumas. He ran every day after class, whether it was 90 degrees or snowing. One day he asked me to come with him.

"Suit up, dog!" he said, using the nickname we shared with Doug and Beth and several other friends. I put on the red jogging suit my grandmother gave me for Christmas and joined him on the porch outside Good Old 109. He led me across B Street, yelling, "Come on, dog," to the path that wound through the tall grasses of the prairie around the reservoir north of town.

My first run ended in slumping defeat before the endorphins had a chance to kick in. But there was Jamie at my door the next day after class saying, "Suit up, dog!" He pulled me a little farther that time, and a little farther still the next, until we were doing a mile a day, then two miles, then four. The day after our first twelve-mile run, he drove me to a store in Mount Pleasant that sold running shoes, and I got a pair of blue Pumas like his.

I gave up sugar and meat and caffeine. I'd show up at the dinner table, bursting with endorphins from the afternoon's run, and stare at the beautiful leaves of spinach in my salad bowl until I couldn't hold back the laughter.

Jamie graduated in the spring of '77, a year before me. We packed his stuff into a U-Haul and drove to his parents' home in Chicago. The last thing he said to me was "Keep running, dog," which was a nice acknowledgment of mutual passion, but hardly necessary.

I spent that brutally hot summer running along the banks of the Fox River near my mom's house in Appleton. I came home soaked head to toe and got in the shower and turned the water to ice cold. My waist went from a size 36 to a size 29 and I had to buy new clothing in the boy's department. When I meditated, it felt like the sunshine of God filling my body.

I kept up the daily run through my senior year at MIU and sporadically for a few years after graduation, but without the motivation of Jamie, the mileage decreased to a point where the endorphin payoff was hardly worth the effort.

I got a job as a programmer and dropped the vegetarian diet for the computer software diet. Debugging my programs late at night, I ate takeout burgers from a bag or forgot to eat entirely. The sweets and the beer returned. My waist hit 36 again and then 38, bigger than I'd ever been.

By the time I arrived back in Iowa, I was a porked-out mess. It wasn't just the extra weight and the accompanying sluggishness and lack of energy. My head was filled with noise. I was angry with everything. Mostly, I was sick of what I'd let myself become. I wanted the mind and body I had when Jamie and I were running through the tall grass.

The phone rang. At least I heard it ring somewhere way off in our room at the Best Western.

I was meditating, but it wasn't the usual twenty minutes of tedium and fidgeting that I'd kept up for decades mostly out of habit. It was the kind of meditation I used to get after coming back from a long, hot run in the Iowa backcountry. My head lolled back and forth as waves of pleasure rolled over my body. No thoughts, no worries. Eventually, even my mantra faded away into pure Being, just like Maharishi said.

The phone rang again and I heard Sarah get out of her chair to answer it.

"Hello," she said. "Oh, hi Roger."

Shit! Roger Patterson, my business partner, wouldn't call unless there was serious karma on the radar.

"Yeah, that sounds important. I'll have him call you."

I spent the rest of my twenty minutes wondering which of several potential horrors would greet me when I opened my eyes.

"You had a call from Roger," Sarah said when she saw me looking at her. She was sitting with her mystery novel on the chair next to the bed. "He says you need to call Gabe at Executive Software Decisions. Their ship date is in two weeks."

"Oh God, no," I groaned.

We checked out early. The desk clerk was a pleasant woman who looked and sounded very midwestern. Sarah asked her how long she'd lived in town.

"Five years. My husband's from here," she said in an upbeat tone as country music played in the background.

"So what do local people think of Maharishi University?" Sarah asked.

"Some of the older ones don't like it, but I guess most of the younger ones are used to it by now. To each his own, I say. As long as they don't try to push their beliefs on me."

On the way out of town, we stopped at Casey's General Store to fill up the tank in the convertible. The woman at the counter wore denim hot pants and a black T-shirt with a picture of a pickup truck shooting flames from its exhaust. Sarah asked her what Fairfield residents thought of Maharishi University.

"We tolerate 'em," she said matter-of-factly.

As we drove north from Fairfield on Highway 1, I told Sarah about something Ron told me.

"He said that there's a lot less tension between the roos and the townies than there used to be. There's a lot more mixing. When you work in the same office with a person day after day, you see that they don't have horns and a tail."

"Harold would have been fascinated by Fairfield," she said, referring to her father, a sociologist who studied human ecology. "He used to talk about minority groups mixing with the larger culture. He always said that assimilation is inevitable. The question isn't whether assimilation is going to occur; it will. The question is when and how."

I switched on the campus radio station, KHOE. "Heaven on Earth," I told my wife. A wooden flute played low, swooping tones as the prairie flashed by.

Sarah was rummaging through a paper bag filled with books, magazines, and pamphlets that I'd acquired in the MUM bookstore.

"There's the Maharishi Vedic Approach to Health," she said. "Maharishi Vedic Management, Maharishi Vedic Astrology."

"Maharishi Vedic Spaghetti," I said, which got a laugh. "Maharishi Vedic Approach to Cosmetic Dentistry."

"The Maharishi Effect?" Sarah asked, as she paged through a booklet of the same name filled with technical charts and diagrams.

"It's a kind of force field," I said. "If you get enough people in one place practicing TM and the sidhis, it creates a big wave of consciousness. It radiates out into the world and brings peace and harmony. Supposedly."

We listened to the flute and watched the scenery for a while.

"The funny thing is that Maharishi used to say that all you need is TM—you meditate for five to eight years and you get enlightened, and that's it. Now you need a Maharishi Vedic house and Maharishi Vedic medicine. You have to meditate together in a big dome to produce the Maharishi Effect. Everything's changed . . . it's like a completely different group. I feel like I'm a total newbie."

"How about your friends?"

"I dunno. Everybody I met seemed okay."

"I thought it was a really friendly place," said Sarah. "Weird, but friendly."

I chuckled. "My grandfather said the same thing when he went there for my graduation in '78. He talked about it for the rest of his life—how everybody was smiling and having a good time. He said that it was the happiest college campus he'd ever seen.

"Twenty years later and they're still there, still having a good time. Maybe they're enlightened or maybe they're just stuck in the sixties. At least they didn't sell out like I did."

As soon as we arrived home in Wisconsin, I got out of the car and went directly to the computer in my office. As I was downloading the latest version of RightSize!, Gabe called in a panic and told me that his product absolutely had to ship by the end of the month.

Sure enough, Boris the programmer had gutted the software and returned to the drawing board, which meant that I had to start over from scratch. I put in an afternoon with the RightSize! tutorial making executive decisions—should I lay off Joe in Accounting or Brenda in Human Resources?—by gingerly tiptoeing around the keystrokes and mouse clicks that sent the program to an early grave.

"I hate this," I told Sarah over dinner. She took my hand and gave me her comforting look.

"When you're ready, you can leave," she said. "You can take a vacation, a sabbatical. Roger would understand if you wanted to quit for good."

For seven days, I never left RightSize! except to sleep and use the bathroom. Gabe called every day and with a rising tone of fear in his voice begged me to work faster. Late on the seventh night, I sent him his manual and training video two steps ahead of the wolf at the door.

With one emergency over, I got back to the projects I'd put on hold: Vegas Employee Manager, Rebel Forms ("Break all the rules of database form design!"), and ULanx ("Your intelligent solution for every kind of content"). Each client told me the same thing: "We have a very aggressive deadline."

⌒

The phone rang and a growly voice cut off my "hello."

"The Dog of Wonder!" He used the college nickname I hadn't heard in decades.

"Doug! The Salty Dog! Hey, man!"

It was six weeks after Sarah and I returned from our aborted visit to Fairfield. I'd met the useless deadline for Executive Software Decisions, like I met all the useless deadlines. Gabe thanked me and disappeared for a month. Then he called to tell me what I already knew, that his program wouldn't ship on schedule. He said he'd get back to me when the new version of the software was ready.

"I heard you were in Fairfield," Doug said.

I smiled into the phone. "Just for a couple days," I said. "I had to leave on short notice. You're still in town?"

"Yeah. I live in Fairfield and I work in Iowa City on the weekends."

We talked and laughed just like old times. After hanging up, I told Sarah that I really wanted to see my old friend. My worst client was on hold and I could afford a couple of days off.

I drove to Iowa City and parked the convertible in the lot behind Medici & Jive, the downtown gallery/coffee shop where Doug worked part time. I found him in a loft hanging pictures on the wall. He was still long and wiry, but his blond hair was going gray. He'd ditched his Movement garb for torn jeans and a black silk jacket. When he saw me, he acted like I'd just stepped out of the room a few minutes ago.

"Hi. C'mon over here and take a look at something," he said, motioning me to a wall with several large canvases. He pointed at the biggest one. It was a landscape—gently rolling farm country of the kind between Fairfield and Iowa City. Two people, a man in dungarees and a woman in a long dress, were flying through the air with their arms outstretched like birds. The guy was carrying a pitchfork.

"American Gothic?" I asked Doug. He nodded.

A red Corvette swooped out of the clouds, apparently in hot pursuit of the farm couple. The car had a vanity license plate that read DOUG.

"It's beautiful," I told him.

We walked downstairs to the coffee shop where the Goth girl at the counter knew Doug's preference for lots of cream and sugar. We sat on a worn leather sofa and did what my old friend called "the catch-up thing."

"I sell a piece now and then. I work here part time. It's a pretty hand-to-mouth existence.

"I tried the real world thing. No, really! I did a year of art school in London. It wasn't going anywhere, and I was thinking about coming back to Fairfield anyway when I heard about the Taste of Utopia course. When I got back into town I thought, 'Oh shit, I'm back where I started,' but it turned out to be the best time I ever had.

"Everybody was there. Every room on campus was full and all of the hotels were packed. It was like a whole enlightened city. When you walked into the dome you got knocked over by the silence. All you had to do was sit on the foam and close your eyes and whoosh! Everybody was saying, 'This is the big one! The Age of Enlightenment!'"

"So you stayed on instead of going back to art school?"

"Yeah. We all figured that the big phase transition would come any day."

We took a few silent sips of coffee. Obviously, the big phase transition never happened.

Doug's car was on the fritz, and he needed to get to Fairfield, so I offered him a ride. He loaded one of his paintings into the back seat of the convertible, a picture of a luminous being with an electric guitar titled *Hendrix, Apotheosis*.

"There's a lot of good stuff going on in Fairfield now," he said as we drove down Highway 1. "Lots of live music, good restaurants, coffee shops . . . it's a totally different place than it was when we lived there."

I made a sour comment about the town getting cultured while the campus deteriorated.

"The Movement's on its last legs," Doug said flatly. "The Utopia course was the high point, and it's been pretty much downhill from there. Everything gets more and more expensive. A lot of the meditators in town are just scraping by. Some leave because they can't make a living and some of them who stay aren't really in the Movement anymore. They may still do TM, but they don't go to the domes, or they don't even meditate anymore."

He turned and gave me a searching look.

"Remember when the Movement was fun?" he asked. I nodded, recalling the late nights when the gang would climb in Doug's car for midnight drives through rural Iowa with the windows down, singing to the corn at the top of our lungs.

"I really miss the excitement," he said.

We drove past the campus and he pointed out Good Old 109.

"When did they paint it gold?" I asked, and Doug shook his head as if he didn't know or care. The building was dull brown in our day, and back then you could still see the faded outlines of the Greek letters from the old Parsons fraternities. There used to be a joke about covering up the Greek with Sanskrit and turning Sigma Delta into Karma Dharma. Now the Movement's gold paint was as faded and peeled as the old Parsons brown.

We arrived downtown, and I helped Doug unload his painting from the back seat.

"So do you ever see Beth?" I asked.

"Not for a couple of years. She was around, but I think she moved back home to Kentucky. Last I heard, she was having some health problems."

We said good-bye and promised to get together again soon. Then I drove back to the university and, on a whim, parked in the crumbling lot of Yagyavalkya Hall, the concrete circle of classrooms that used to be called the Learning Center.

From the little I'd read about the subject, the LC violated every rule of Maharishi Architecture. Round instead of square. No windows. Doors facing promiscuously in every direction, auspicious or not.

I tried a door and found it open, so I walked in and switched on the lights. It was the main lecture hall, a wedge-shaped auditorium with tiered rows of desks. In my day, the front of the room had a blackboard and podium for faculty lectures. They were gone, replaced by a monumental portrait of Guru Dev flanked by garlands of flowers and blue silk hangings. He looked out contentedly at the silent room with its hundreds of empty desks.

I turned off the lights and went back outside to continue my walk around the building's perimeter, pausing at a familiar spot with a good view of the whole campus. Below me, a field of several acres separated the historic Parsons campus to the south from the domes and the student housing to the north.

I remembered standing on the same spot twenty years ago when I was working on the university video crew. It was a celebration, one of the Movement's anniversaries or inaugurations or other special events that seemed to fall out of the blue sky along with a directive to put on nice clothes and assemble for speeches and a group photo, followed by cookies and milk.

I recalled standing under the concrete awning of the Learning Center with my video camera, peering through the viewfinder down at the field where hundreds of people were looking back up at me and waving to Maharishi.

I looked up and shrugged off the faces of the crowd. "Every single inch of this place has a memory," I thought.

As I was walking back to the car, I noticed a group of women coming out of the chapel on the old quad. The door had been locked when Sarah and I were exploring the campus. After Good Old 109, the chapel was my favorite building on campus, the one with the best memories. I walked through the door I last entered on my graduation day two decades earlier.

It was a small sanctuary with a high, arched ceiling supported by rows of wooden beams. The old pews with their green cushions were lined up just as they were during my graduation ceremony. I sat in one of the pews and looked up at a stained glass window. The image—an intricate mosaic of Jesus and his disciples—brought back the memory of my surprise birthday party.

It was the year I turned twenty. The day went by as usual, with classes, meditation, and curried tofu for dinner. In the evening, there was a piano recital in the chapel by Paul Jones, one of the music professors. Fifty or so students sat in the pews and listened to Paul play "Pictures at an Exhibition" brilliantly and from memory on the chapel's grand piano.

Afterward, as the audience applauded, somebody went up to Paul and said, "It's Geoff Gilpin's birthday." He walked over to the keyboard of the chapel's pipe organ, flipped on the power, and played "Happy Birthday" full blast with great bravado. A couple of the kitchen staff brought in cake and ice cream as the last organ notes faded away. People gave me comic books, a jar of instant coffee, some sandalwood incense, and a toy gun that shot ping-pong balls. Everybody was smiling. I'd never been on the receiving end of so much affection before.

I sat in my pew, balancing my piece of cake on a paper plate and looking up at the stained glass window where Christ and his disciples glowed in the sunset. It was the happiest day of my life.

The gray stone walls of Parsons Hall, one of the original buildings on the Parsons College campus, rose in the 1870s and held their ground for the ninety-nine-year history of the school. They stood by as the old alma mater declined and perished and the student body packed up their Pink Floyd albums and caught the last Greyhound bus out of Iowa.

When the Movement occupied the campus, Maharishi's senior administrators moved in to the wood-paneled offices in Parsons, Carnegie, and Fairfield Halls. In 1983, thanks to the efforts of the MIU administration, Parsons Hall, Barhydt Chapel, and several other buildings on the old quad were placed on the National Register of Historic Places.

Along with protecting the old buildings from incursion by Highway 1 or other unwanted development, the university made some much-needed renovations to the aging campus. They restored the historic Henn building to its turn-of-the-century glory. They renovated the pond in the middle of campus, dredging its stagnant water and turning it into a sparkling showpiece.

In 1989, Maharishi's Year of Heaven on Earth, the guru added several of the traditional Vedic sciences to his curriculum. These included Ayurveda, Indian traditional medicine, Jyotish, Vedic astrology, and Sthapatya Veda, the ancient codes of construction and landscaping set down by Indian seers thousands of years ago.

Along with the taboo about southern entrances, the rules of Sthapatya Veda forbid water to the south of inhabited buildings. That meant the death penalty for the pond, which was entombed by landfill, transforming the middle of campus into a swamp.

In May of 2000, a crew of men with heavy equipment rolled onto the old quad and reduced Parsons Hall to a hole in the ground. Carnegie Hall met the same fate in July.

Back home in Wisconsin, I received a "dear alumni" letter from my alma mater in Fairfield. The enclosed brochure, entitled "Maharishi's Inspiration for Removing Obstacles to Our Progress," explained the situation on campus.

"Maharishi recently asked the faculty to imagine what they would do if all the unfortunate old buildings which are not in accord with Natural Law had been destroyed by a hurricane.

"These buildings have features that are in violation of the Laws of Nature, primarily improper orientation. As such, they create an improper relationship with the intelligence that organizes the universe and thus create unseen obstacles to our progress.

"If a hurricane destroyed these buildings, Maharishi pointed out, we would relocate the people and functions that were in those buildings to other buildings. So why not do that now—that is, close all the old buildings we can and redouble our focus on demolishing them?"

The brochure featured a picture of Maharishi, bathed in a golden nimbus above a quote in big letters:

"Demolition is the technique for gaining support of Natural Law."

There was a photo of a Fairfield couple who donated $13,000 to the university's demolition fund, posing outside one of the condemned buildings. The gentleman manned the controls of a backhoe. The lady, sledgehammer poised to strike, wore a hard hat and a long, flowing, spotlessly white skirt. A sidebar noted "These simple measures will remove great obstacles to the university's success and good fortune . . ."

I added the brochure to my Tyvek envelope of Movement oddities and got back to work in my home office. I fired up ULanx, the software that my latest client claimed would organize everything on my hard drive, which it might if it ever went beyond its current state of a single, blank screen that did nothing.

After an hour or so of attempting to spin straw into gold, I left the computer and went downstairs to the living room and opened the front door of our house, which faces southeast. I walked out onto the porch and stared into the distant corn fields.

What is out there? I thought. It's almost as if poverty, disease, and mental instability were actual, solid things. Terrorists, home invaders, lurking out there waiting to sneak in if the front door faced the wrong way.

Back at MIU in the seventies, people sometimes talked about demons, *rakshasas* in Sanskrit. Demons are a fixture of Indian religion and folklore. As such, most Movement people believe in them even though they're not part of Maharishi's official curriculum. At least they weren't part of it back then.

If somebody were to ask you about your Yogic Flying practice: Doesn't this violate Newton's law of gravity? The first thing that you should say is that Newton's law is a nineteenth-century law."

"Ha!" Sarah chortled. We were sitting in our family room watching a video titled *The Physics of Flying.*

"Yogic Flying, the ability of the body to float and fly, really demonstrates mastery over the gravitational force."

The man on the video spoke in calmly measured tones, clearly enunciating each word. He seemed boyish and professorial at the same time.

". . . the principles of quantum mechanics pertain to the same levels of abstract thinking that the meditating mind experiences daily."

The camera panned over an audience of clean-cut meditators. They listened intently, although none of them appeared to be taking notes.

"If you can take the awareness to deeper levels of natural law, then by transcending the classical laws of nature, which are really statistical laws based on quantum mechanical principles, you can gain mastery over those classical laws."

Sarah leaned over to me. "Who is this guy?" she asked.

"Maharishi's latest and greatest," I replied.

". . . by functioning consciously at the microscopic level . . . you can upset the statistical laws of averaging that ordinarily give rise to the classical expectation known as Einstein's theory, and give rise to any desired shape in the gravitational field. So that, instead of falling down, which is the most probable outcome, the body will fall up."

Scientology recruits movie stars.

Reverend Moon recruits politicians.

Maharishi recruits nerds.

Guys in lab coats. Physicists. Mathematicians. Neurophysiologists. If you've got a freshly minted Ph.D. in quantum mechanics—preferably from a place like Harvard or MIT—the Movement has exciting job opportunities. You might also be surprised at how many of your colleagues have signed on.

The first batch of scientists to enter Maharishi's orbit included a couple of celebrities: Buckminster Fuller, the mathematician who invented the geodesic dome, and Brian Josephson, the Nobel Prize–winning physicist. Neither of them stuck around long, and Maharishi never snagged another big name, but he's been pulling in qualified talent ever since.

What does a guru need with an R&D department? In the early days— back when TM was the whole focus of the Movement—the answer was clear. Maharishi knew that scientific proof would be a big draw for a Western audience.

The breakthrough came in the late sixties when one of Maharishi's followers—a young Harvard neuroscientist named Robert Keith Wallace— glued electrodes onto the scalps of test subjects who did TM. He recorded their EEG patterns in and out of meditation. He analyzed their blood chemistry. He measured their breathing and heart rate and the ability of their skin to conduct electricity.

Then he published, and not just in some Movement newsletter. His first article appeared in *Science*—as prestigious as it gets—in 1970. More Wallace articles appeared in *Scientific American* and the *American Journal of Physiology*. The national and international media picked up the news that TM improves your physical and mental health.

If you attended a TM lecture in the early seventies, you got the same little booklet of scientific charts that I got in Green Bay. Every page had a chart or graph with titles like "Increased Resistance to Diseases," "Decreased Anxiety," "Normalized Blood Pressure," and "Improved Academic Performance." It was brilliant publicity. There's no doubt that the work of Dr. Wallace and other Movement scientists had a lot to do with the success of TM.

What's more, their research blazed a trail that many others followed, a trail that led way beyond TM and the Movement. The field has produced tons of literature and research grants and solid evidence. Meditation— formerly unknown outside the worlds of spirituality and religion—is now part of the scientific and medical mainstream. Your doctor will prescribe it and your HMO will pay for you to learn it in a class at a nearby hospital or YMCA.

All of this might have happened eventually without Maharishi, but he started it. The scientific study of spiritual matters may be his single greatest legacy.

There was a period in the seventies when scientific research was the most important thing in the Movement. It turned up everywhere in the MIU curriculum. You'd be in a lit class and the professor would talk about romantic poetry and brain wave coherence. I thought it was too much, but I didn't say anything."

"Because you wanted to keep a low profile?" asked Sarah. The Yogic Flying video was over and the only light in our family room came from the fireplace.

"Yeah, and part of me wanted it to be true. I really liked the idea that science and mysticism could go together, and nobody was talking about that except Maharishi. But after a while I started getting skeptical."

Maharishi predicted that the TM-Sidhi Program—Yogic Flying— would have a much more dramatic effect than plain TM. And not just on the people who practiced it, but society as a whole. To test the theory, he ordered large groups of sidhas to assemble in cities around the world and dispatched teams of his scientists to study the consequences. They collected mountains of data, subjected them to advanced methods of statistical analysis, and, when all the numbers were crunched, announced a revolutionary discovery. The Maharishi Effect is the ability of humans to directly influence physical reality—even at great distances—through meditation.

"This is the study they're really proud of," I said, digging through the stacks of literature I'd collected on the topic. "The experiment happened in Jerusalem in the late eighties. A group of sidhas got together to practice Yogic Flying every day. The researchers monitored the size of the group and a bunch of other statistics like traffic accidents in Israel and war deaths in Lebanon."[3]

I showed Sarah a graph with two lines. When the number of Yogic Flyers went up, the number of people who died in the war went down.

I pulled out other charts and graphs that demonstrated the power of the Maharishi Effect. Stock prices rose in Britain and Australia. Violent crime, traffic fatalities, suicides, unemployment, inflation, and terrorist incidents declined in cities around the world. Relations between the United States and the Soviet Union improved. When the number of Yogic Flyers fell, everything went to hell again.[4]

"So you can have a group of people in Fairfield bouncing on foam mats, and that makes the crime rate in England go down," said Sarah in her contrarian voice.

"That's what they're saying. In a way, it's just the traditional Indian idea that everything is connected. Your individual consciousness is part of the global consciousness. When you do TM and the sidhis, the whole universe responds."

"So the stock market goes up," said Sarah.

I grinned. "Yeah, it can get pretty far out there. They had one paper called 'The Effect of Coherent Collective Consciousness on the Weather.' They claimed that Yogic Flyers make the winters in Iowa warmer."

Sarah grimaced.

"I doubt that anybody outside the Movement takes this seriously," I said. "Most people have never heard of it. But if you're in the Movement, it's a scientific revolution greater than Galileo and Einstein put together. The Maharishi Effect is the end of traditional science. Nothing else matters."

"Except it's nuts," said Sarah.

"I *think* it's nuts, but I don't *know* it's nuts. Check out the articles. They look just like the stuff you see in *Scientific American*—all the math and jargon look authentic. And Maharishi's people are the real thing.

"This guy on the videotape—John Hagelin. He has a Ph.D. in physics from Harvard and he's a big gun in quantum theory. He obviously believes in the Maharishi Effect and he's got the credentials to back it up. I don't know, maybe he's deluding himself. Either that . . . or he's right."

I was buried in ULanx when Gabe called with the good news that he'd actually managed to bring his product to market. He sent me a copy of the manual per our contract. I opened it, thumbed through a few pages, saw what had become of my work, and cursed out loud.

There were still a few paragraphs of my writing here and there, interspersed with stuff like this:

"If you choose to purchase Chinese factory, first enter factory parameters chosen, such as desired units, and then enter factory purchase choice, such as Chinese, and then press button 'Decide' and then choose Chinese Factory."

I phoned Executive Software Decisions.

"Gabe, did you give Boris permission to rewrite the manual?"

"Well . . . he's the programmer. He said he thought your verbiage was unclear."

I gripped the phone tighter.

"Gabe, he . . . can't . . . speak . . . English!"

"Well, I know. But he's the programmer."

For the first time in my decades-long, fairly successful, reasonably well-paying career in the computer software industry, I called one of my clients a fucking asshole and slammed the phone down on him.

Then, finally, I cried.

"Are you ready to leave yet?" Sarah asked over dinner.

"I'm getting there," I said.

Unfolded, the Constitution of the Universe took up a good chunk of my office floor. On the left side of the poster, under the little picture of Maharishi, were columns and rows of Sanskrit words from the Vedas. On the right side, in matching columns and rows, mathematical equations from quantum mechanics. Two ways of describing consciousness. Two ways of writing the same thing, matched up one-to-one, syllable to formula. If you master the Vedic mantras, you can control the laws of quantum mechanics and create any reality you want.

Despite my ignorance of Sanskrit and physics, the poster looked familiar. Back at MIU, Maharishi had us prepare similar charts. We'd get a list of his latest buzzwords ("invincibility," "fullness," "self-reference") and a list of topics in, say, Biology ("thyroid," "neurotransmitter," "DNA") and instructions to find the correlations. The Constitution of the Universe looked like a similar exercise undertaken by a committee of Ph.D.s.

As I stared at the esoteric symbols, an uncomfortable tingly sensation formed at the base of my spine—the nagging twinge I get when I want to understand something that's just beyond my grasp.

Maybe it's because I grew up in a family of scientists. My mom and dad, my grandparents, my uncle—they knew calculus, physics, chemistry, the whole shebang. At the very least, I should be able to tell if something like the Constitution of the Universe or the Maharishi Effect is real science or a clever fraud or empty nonsense.

I should, but I couldn't. I felt helpless.

You know, a lot of the time I think that the Movement's nuts. But it's healthier than the software business. And the people in it stayed true to their beliefs. They didn't sell out."

I looked over the dinner table at Sarah and I knew right away that something I'd said pissed her off.

"You've been complaining about how you sold out for as long as I've known you," she said. "It's getting old." She pushed her plate away and gave me a hard stare.

"And you've been obsessed with the Movement all along, even though you don't talk about it. You say you meditate out of habit and because you've got a stressful job. But if I ask you to stay up after ten or do something at five when you're supposed to be meditating, you get huffy and defensive.

"Remember when we drove onto the MIU campus and you realized you were wearing jeans? You were hyperventilating. That wasn't the reaction of somebody who was afraid of making a faux pas. That was the reaction of somebody who was afraid of getting hit by lightning."

She softened a bit and took my hand.

"You've obviously got some unfinished business back there. Some soul-searching or *something*. I think it would be *really* good for you to sort it out."

I thought it over for a minute. "Well," I said, "the Movement research is bugging me. The Maharishi Effect. It's like a gray area between science and religion. If I could figure out which it is, it might be an important test case. There could be an article in it."

Sarah smiled. "You know how busy I am right now," she said. "I've got enough work to keep me tied up for at least a month. I'll hardly notice that you're gone."

A few days after I sent off the ULanx material, my business partner, Roger, called to tell me about a prospective client.

"Their product is called NanoMerge, 'the total solution for the rest of us.' They asked for you personally. The one thing is that . . . they have a very aggressive deadline."

"Uh, Roger, there's something we have to discuss."

Chapter 6

The Department of Development of Consciousness

Please take off your shoes," said the proprietress of the old Victorian boarding house. With her lacy dress and air of propriety, she could have been an innkeeper in a Dickens novel.

"Would you like a cookie?" she asked, picking up a plate of them from an end table covered with an ornate doily. "I bake them fresh every day and put them out for the tenants."

She led Sarah and me across a worn carpet and up a flight of creaking stairs. "There's only one room left," she said. "I'm afraid that the door faces west."

Aside from the bad-luck entrance and an uneven floor, the room was tidy and old-fashioned with lace curtains and cut-glass sconces that could have been gas jets.

"So why didn't you take it?" Sarah asked as we stepped out into the crisp autumn air.

"I'm an adult now. I need my own bathroom. Besides, if I lived there I'd develop an opium habit."

We climbed into Sarah's Saturn and I picked up the copy of the *Fairfield Weekly Reader* with the real estate ads I'd circled.

"There's one over on Second. '2 Bedroom Apt. Furnished. Washer/Dryer. East Entrance.' You can tell the roo landlords."

"Yeah," said Sarah. "They're . . . sweet."

We drove past the apartment building on Second, saw the dilapidated porch and sagging roof, and didn't stop. I read another ad in the *Weekly Reader*.

"Come to the Homes by the Domes! Utopia Park, where the living is easy. Just a short walk from the Golden Dome."

We had to see it. Sarah drove through the university past the old frat houses to the edge of campus.

"This used to be a cornfield," I said. It was now a trailer park. The sign at the entrance said:

TASTE OF UTOPIA STREET

"It's more like Tobacco Road," said Sarah as we meandered through the warren of scruffy trailers. She turned a corner and swerved to avoid a skinny guy in an off-white suit on a bicycle. As we drove away from campus, I took a pen and drew an X through the ad for Utopia Park. Then I looked up and saw a golden spire capped by an onion-shaped dome shining high above the trailer park.

"It's . . . a house?" asked Sarah, as the building under the spire rose before us. It was a humongous mansion—part Babylonian, part Beverly Hillbillies, all Maharishi. If Krishna picked it up and set it down next door it would flatten half the trailer homes in Utopia Park.

Sarah stopped by the main entrance and we silently wondered at the many-layered Vedic ziggurat. Although a big fence concealed a lot of the property, I could see the summit of an artificial mountain that might be part of a water park or miniature golf course. We drove off, amazed.

After a few more unsuitable apartments, Sarah dropped me off downtown for a lunch date with Doug. He'd asked me to meet him at a coffeehouse off the square called Revelations, which I loved the minute I walked in. It smelled of coffee and baked goods. There was interesting art on the walls and comfortable people sitting at the tables talking intently or tapping at their computers. I felt at home.

I found Doug seated by a rack of free newspapers.

"This place is just like Madison," I said as I took a seat next to him.

"It's hard to believe you're in Fairfield," he said. "There's good coffee, too." I ordered chicken salad on whole wheat and Doug got espresso with a cruller. As we ate, I asked him about the trailer park.

"They built it around the time of the Taste of Utopia course. If you were out there you must have seen the Kaplan place."

"The big mansion? That's Earl Kaplan?" I asked.

Doug nodded. "What did you think of it?" I grinned and laughed and he seemed pleased. "You should see it at night when it's all lit up," he said.

He threw back his espresso as a young woman in bright blue leotards and a candy-striped jacket strolled by our table. The crowd was a mixture of the young and hip with the middle-aged and sedate. The boomers had the lean and shiny look of lifelong vegetarians. One guy wore the cream-colored suit of a Movement insider, but most could pass at a Starbucks in Wisconsin. They wore slacks and sweaters and they talked to their kids on their cell phones.

"So you're apartment hunting," Doug said. "I knew it. It's like a revolving door here. You guys'll fit right in."

"It's just me, not Sarah. Just for a little while." Doug gave me a broad, conspiratorial grin. He didn't ask why I was moving back to Fairfield. In fact, I only heard that question once the whole time I was there. Even people who left the Movement on bad terms seemed to assume that moving to Fairfield was a mark of common sense.

We were discussing dessert when a bright look came over Doug's face. He reached into the pocket of his Army surplus jacket and pulled out a CD with a silver banana on the cover.

"Have you heard the Velvet Underground reunion album?" he asked. That was it; we spent the next hour talking about music. From time to time I glanced up and saw other roo-types lingering over coffee and reading or talking quietly. Revelations was a little outpost of café society in the great broad plains.

As the shadows lengthened, I told Doug I needed to get serious about finding an apartment.

"Try this one," he said, pointing to an ad in the *Weekly Reader*. I called the number in the ad and got an Indian woman, yet another Lakshmi.

"I need a place to stay while I'm in town on business," I explained. "Would you consider a month-to-month lease?"

"How many months?" Lakshmi asked.

"Two."

"Only two months! Oh!" She sounded like I'd stuck her with a pin. "Oh, well . . . I have to talk to my husband." I heard an anxious conversation in the background.

"Hello?" she said. "Well . . . if you need a place to stay, we won't turn you away."

Doug and I drove to the little house near campus and retrieved the key from a milk can by the front door.

"Wow," said Doug when we walked in. Everything was clean and tidy. The furniture was solid and the appliances were mostly new. "You don't see rental property like this often," Doug said. "This is the place."

On the day I moved in, I discovered fresh flowers and a jar of home-made jam on the dining room table. I learned later that Lakshmi's husband, Randy, had been a member of the Thousand-Headed Purusha, Maharishi's elite unit of celibate monks. He left his guru's service when he met the woman of his dreams.

The morning after my arrival, I woke up, showered, meditated, and drove to Revelations for a muffin and coffee.

Some time around my third cup, I looked up from the *New York Times*, savored the caffeinated fizz in my head, and thought of poor Roger back in the office fighting off hopeless clients and their software that never worked. I tried to think of one reason why I should go back to that, and failed.

Two women at the next table were talking about organic apricots. Their conversation gave them away as roos, but I would have known anyway. Movement people—at least the ones who frequent the coffee shops—look really healthy for baby boomers. They're all in their late forties/early fifties, same as me, but they look younger. The faces at the next table were clear and smooth and relaxed, the product of decades of healthy food and sound sleep. My reflection in the table's glass top looked dark, puffy, and old. Compared to the people who stayed on in Fairfield, I looked like a wreck.

It was time to get back on the program. The diet of the last twenty years had to go. Fortunately, Fairfield is a great place to eat healthy.

I did most of my shopping at Everybody's, the organic grocery store near campus. Unlike the HyVee, Everybody's makes no concession to middle-Iowan tastes. The roo customers are as serious about food as it gets.

(Sometimes *too* serious. I remember people at MIU telling me that a single drop of artificial dye or one taste of animal protein would block the experience of pure bliss consciousness and set back enlightenment. There were several fad diets, including the mucus-free diet and the all milk diet.)

Like Revelations, Everybody's is the kind of high-quality establishment you'd expect to find in a large city. The produce comes right from the farm and the goods in bottles and boxes are handcrafted in small batches by people who give a damn. I loved wandering up and down the aisles, admiring the gourmet cheeses and the bins of grain and the bulging granola cookies. No wonder the roos look healthy.

Everybody's is like Revelations in another way—it's one part store and two parts social nexus. You go to pick up two pounds of bulk basmati rice and you linger with friends to discuss the evolution of consciousness or the new movie at the Co-Ed.

One morning at Everybody's, as I picked up a jar of cashew butter, I noticed a couple of sixtyish, white-haired guys pushing carts ahead of me in the aisle. In that unfamiliar context, it took me a second to recognize them as two of the original MIU faculty members.

God, how we worshipped those guys. We used to have arguments about their respective levels of consciousness.

"Paul's in God Consciousness."

"No, Michael's in *God* Consciousness, Paul's in *Unity* Consciousness."

Now here they were, decades later, Unity Consciousness or not, pushing shopping carts past the jars of nut butter.

I went to the Fairfield Transcendental Meditation Center (a room in the Dreier Building on campus) to apply for an ID card. Without a badge, you can't get into the dome or participate in any official activities. Heck, you can hardly meditate, at least in any way that counts. Solitary meditation in your house or hotel room is like spilling your seed on the desert floor—it doesn't generate the Maharishi Effect, so it doesn't count.

The TM center director was a tall, lean woman in an ankle-length dress named Melinda. She was about the same age as Ron and Sheila and Doug and me and everybody else in that place—the cohort who arrived in the seventies and early eighties and stayed on to follow the dream to its conclusion.

"What was the name of your initiator?" she asked.

"Uh . . . Harry. I don't remember his last name."

"Well, that may be a bit of a problem. We may be able to find his name in the database."

The famous Movement records. What else would they find out about me in there? Some character defect that would make me unfit for the Golden Dome?

As Melinda worked on my application form, I made a quick mental inventory of my sins. I once told a guy in my dorm that "you have to take everything that Maharishi says with a grain of salt." Did that get into my file? Would it be cause for . . . for what? I remembered the paranoid stories from the old days.

"They keep an eye on you," Ron said. A group of us were sitting in his room after-hours. A single lamp burned. We stared at Ron like campers enthralled by a counselor telling the story of the serial killer with a hook for a hand. "You want to keep a low profile," Ron said. "If you get a bad rep they ban you from any new courses."

Everyone looked at Ron with big eyes. He was talking about the biggest fear in the Movement—losing access to Maharishi and any new secrets he might reveal. It was like shunning for the Amish, except worse—the loss of enlightenment, a kind of spiritual death.

"Are you moving back to Fairfield permanently?" Melinda asked in a pleasant voice.

"No, just temporarily."

"Could you tell me the reason for your visit?"

"Uh, sure." That's a good question. Unfinished business? A burning need to find out what the hell happened to the Movement? One last desperate attempt to discover some meaning in a wasted life?

"Research," I said. "I'm a writer."

"Oh," said Melinda. "You'll fit right in. There are tons of writers here."

I didn't have any running shoes, so I put on an old pair of Keds sneakers and walked down B Street to the path where Jamie brought me the first day we went running. There wasn't much for joggers back then, just a foot path tamped down in the tall grasses of the prairie around the reservoir north of town.

I was delighted that the path was now a broad, smooth trail covered with a bed of wood chips that were soft to my old feet. The trail wound through cool groves of trees past thickets of Queen Anne's Lace curling up for the end of the year. The reservoir sparkled. It was cleaner and bluer and much more inviting than it was in the seventies. The City of Fairfield obviously put a lot of effort into the place.

As I ran along the trail, I took a mental inventory of all the items in my bygone spiritual life. TM twice a day. Running. Vegetarianism. Early to bed.

I passed a hardcore runner in an MUM T-shirt with a grin on his face that was either Cosmic Consciousness or the world's champion endorphin rush.

"So," I thought, "what would it take to get serious about enlightenment? What more would I have to do?"

To be as serious as my old friends who stayed in Fairfield, I'd have to give up everything else. Or at least put it all on the back burner. I'd need a rigorous spiritual program in an understanding, supportive community. Would I have to leave Wisconsin and move back to Iowa?

More importantly, what would I have to believe?

I thought about those things for a half mile or so, until my arches started to hurt and I quit running. But I was back the next day.

Melinda phoned to say that my badge was ready. I reported back to the Dreier Building and she handed me a laminated ID card. The photo showed me wide-eyed and smiling beneath my new title:

CITIZEN OF THE AGE OF ENLIGHTENMENT

"So . . . do I meditate in the dome now?" I asked Melinda.

"Oh, no. You can go to the dome for special events, but only sidhas meditate there. You'll be meditating with other citizens."

For my meditation assignment, Melinda sent me to the Department of Development of Consciousness, an office in the student union. I met a friendly woman named Margie whose job title was Director of Research in Consciousness.

"I try to make sure that everybody has a comfortable place to meditate," she said. "The Dreier Building is too small to accommodate all the meditating students at once, so we have three shifts in the morning and three in the evening."

Margie handed me a sheet of paper with a matrix of schedules, one for men and one for women.

"It's a lot more structured than it used to be," I said.

"Yes," she replied simply. I thought I detected a bit of a wistful sigh.

I looked over the list of rules for the meditation halls. Under the dress-code section, I noticed that women were prohibited from wearing dresses with spaghetti straps.

At 4:55 p.m., I reported to the Dreier Building for my first group meditation. I joined a line of young men wearing suits and ties with no shoes waiting outside the meditation room. They looked to be Middle Eastern, African, Indian, East Asian . . . everything except the middle-class Caucasians who made up the MIU student body in my day.

Eventually, another white guy appeared and took charge—a stereotypical roo, lean and balding in a light suit with a bland smile. He took his station behind a desk at the head of the line, unlocked a box with an electronic card reader, and motioned for the procession to begin. Each citizen swiped his card through the scanner and proceeded into the meditation hall.

The room had several rows of identical high-backed chairs facing east, the correct direction for meditation according to the codes of Maharishi Architecture. I took a seat next to a tall Asian guy. Since the rules for the meditation hall included total silence, the only sound was sniffling and shuffling.

When the room was full, the hall monitor entered, still wearing his bland smile, and took his seat at the front of the room. He rang a small bell and the thirty or so citizens in the identical high-backed chairs closed their eyes and began the practice of Transcendental Meditation.

The bell rang again twenty minutes later. I slowly opened my eyes and smiled at the high-backed chairs, the dim afternoon light, and the rows of heads nodding around me. I relished the deep silence that began in me and extended seamlessly into the room and outside to the whole world.

My fellow citizens shuffled and opened their eyes and left their chairs one by one. We walked into the hall, smiling at one another without saying a word.

The next time I saw Melinda, I asked her about the people I was meditating with. She told me that they were foreign graduate students studying computer science.

"TM is part of the curriculum for them. They get graded based on attendance at their group program."

"Wow," I said, raising my eyebrows, "that's a big change. Back when I was here, everybody pretty much meditated on their own whenever they felt like it."

"Don't let the students hear you say that," she said with a smile. "Back then I suppose everybody knew what they were here for. For some of the students now, it's just something they have to do as part of their class work."

I recalled something Ron said. He told me that a lot of the foreign students didn't care about TM and certainly weren't interested in Yogic Flying or any of the other Movement stuff. They were looking for an American college degree and a job.

"Of course," Melinda continued, "they get the benefits of meditating regardless of what they believe. They say things like 'It makes you less angry.'"

Did I ever tell you about the time Maharishi came to campus?" Sarah shook her head. I was spending the weekend with her in Wisconsin. We sat by the fire in our family room, a bowl of popcorn and a bottle of Merlot between us.

"Everything went nuts. It was like Beatlemania—there were crowds running back and forth across campus following Maharishi wherever he went. I got freaked out by the herd mentality and I stayed in my room most of the time.

"Anyway, one evening I went out to the student union. The lobby was empty except for a guy I knew from my dorm named Benny. He was sitting on a couch just staring off into space. At first I thought it was weird, but then I realized that something was going on. Something in the lobby felt different, like the whole room was filled with peace and silence. It was really overwhelming and it felt really really good.

"I knew why Benny was just sitting there—he was soaking it up and enjoying it. I sat down next to him and we stayed there for a long time. We didn't have to talk because we knew what we were both feeling.

"I heard some voices coming from the student union banquet hall and I noticed this sign by the door that said:

RESERVED FOR MIU TRUSTEE DINNER

"Benny said 'Maharishi's in there. The most enlightened beings on the planet are in that room.' I thought, 'So that's it!' The highest consciousness in the world, just behind that door. Of course you'd feel it!"

Sarah took a sip of wine and gave me a hard stare.

"I know that's purely subjective," I said, "but it seemed as real as anything. I had a direct experience of consciousness jumping from person to person through walls."

"That's what you believed at the time. You all took it for granted that things like that happen. You were expecting it and you got what you expected."

"Yeah, I suspect you're right." I washed down a handful of popcorn with Merlot. "But I can't ignore it. And everybody in the Movement has similar experiences. That's why they all believe in the Maharishi Effect. It's not just the research studies and the statistics . . . for all I know, they make that stuff up. But everyone has the experience.

"I had it again when I was meditating with the foreign students. It was the deepest meditation I've had in ages. I don't know why it's better with the group . . ."

"Sounds like a self-fulfilling prophecy. A placebo."

I gave Sarah a big grin. "That's why I married you," I said. "There's no reason to believe it was anything more than a placebo. No ooga-booga required."

"Hmm," she said, turning her attention to the popcorn. "I can understand people feeling good after a group meditation. But it's a long way from feeling good to making the stock market go up and down."

I nodded. "It's fascinating. The Maharishi Effect, the whole sidhi thing—flying, invisibility—it's all totally irrational. You can't believe it unless you toss out the last two hundred years of science and reason. But there's this whole town that believes it as much as they believe in computers or TV.

"There's a kind of purity or integrity . . . it's like they're totally uncorrupted by the mundane world. And most of them seem totally sane, saner than a lot of the people in the software business."

Sarah gave me a probing stare.

"Keep your crap detector turned up on high," she said.

By eight p.m. on Friday night, I understood that Fairfield's monthly Art Walk was more like a big party than a gallery tour. The town square was full of people—thousands I'd guess.

I poked my way through the crowd in Revelations, guarding my cup of iced coffee from stray elbows. From the vicinity of the pizza oven, I heard a guy talking about the *Star Wars* film at the Co-Ed. I recognized the voice—rapid, low, penetrating—before I saw one of the best-known faces in the Movement. He was holding forth in a circle of smiling friends, just like I remembered him.

"Dennis Raimondi?" I asked. He grinned wide and shook my hand and we spent the rest of the evening doing the Art Walk together.

As we left Revelations, a five-piece rock band was tuning up on the sidewalk and a crowd was forming in the street. I asked Dennis if he'd been in Fairfield all along.

"Pretty much. I moved to Fairfield in '75 to work for the university. I was the Dean of Students for several years and then I was the Headmaster at the Maharishi school on campus."

In his role as Dean, Dennis knew everybody who passed through MIU, which was pretty much everyone in the Movement back then. As Headmaster, he probably knows a good chunk of the second generation. His own daughter graduated from the Maharishi School of the Age of Enlightenment in 1999.

"I left the university in 1984 and went into business. I moved to Cambridge in 2000 to get a degree at Harvard and I wasn't intending to move back to Fairfield. But I like the community. There's the culture of Iowa, which I really like, and laid on that is the TM community culture."

I asked him how the town had changed since I left.

"Around 1978, there was this big course that Maharishi conducted at the University of Massachusetts in Amherst. After that course, Maharishi encouraged everybody there—and there were several thousand—to pick up and move to Fairfield.

"So in a short period of time, a town of ten thousand, which had maybe fifteen hundred living on campus as students and faculty, had another two thousand moving into town. But they weren't the typical immigrants to Iowa, they were mostly from the East and West Coasts. They moved here in *spite* of the fact that it was Iowa.

"It attracted a lot of entrepreneurial types who started a lot of businesses. Most of them didn't succeed, of course, but there are some big successes. It's a real entrepreneurial paradise—oil brokerage, software. I'm in a video conferencing business. There's a good labor pool. It's one of those places like Aspen, Colorado, where you have highly overqualified people who are willing to work below their level of expertise just so that they can live in the community.

"When the meditators came here, we were so isolated on the university campus, but there's been good integration. A lot of it had to do with the kids, because the kids just don't care. There are plenty of meditator kids in the public school, in the Little League. There was some name-calling at first, but that's all over. There's been a good integration.

"Ed Malloy, the mayor, is a meditator. I think when he first ran it was an issue. People thought, 'Oh, they're trying to take over the town,' but now that he's in, people have seen that he's not prejudiced. He's just a regular mayor and he's pretty popular. I don't think they can even find anybody who wants to run against him.

"It used to be easy to spot the meditators in Fairfield, but now if I see somebody walking down the street, a lot of the time I can't tell if they're meditators or non-meditators or somebody who used to be a meditator. It's just not a big thing anymore."

We walked the circumference of the square past jugglers, a jazz band, bored punk kids, and a bride and groom getting married in the gazebo.

"There's a huge creative community here," Dennis told me. "Music. Art. At one point there were five theater groups."

Dennis knew them all. As we made our circuit of the square, he introduced me to an artist known as the "American Monet," and an architect, dressed in black from head to toe, who started a group called the Foundation for Consciousness in Architecture.

The sun went down and rows of white and colored lights appeared to outline the false fronts of the old buildings on the square. Dennis told me that he was off to meet some friends for a movie. Before we parted, I asked him if he planned to remain in Fairfield.

"I think so. There are things I miss about the city, but I really like it here.

"Last year I hurt my back pretty badly, and if I'd been in New York I'd have been up the creek. But here, people brought me coffee, brought me lunch, gave me rides.

"I have a very close friend. He has cancer and he's been fighting it for five years now. He was living on the East Coast, but he came back here because his community is here. People drop off food at his house, they visit, they help with his financial needs. That happens all the time here. You do that for people, even if you don't know them so well, because they're part of your community."

We shook hands and he walked off in the direction of the Co-Ed Theatre. I wandered back toward Revelations, where the band—the Flapjaw

Larry Project—was playing an irresistible song that mixed psychedelia and surf music with the chorus "Let's all get naked."

A crowd was dancing in the street. It's the kind of scene I come upon in downtown Madison all the time. There, however, it's all college kids and I'm the only one over thirty who isn't at home in front of the TV. The Flapjaw Larry crowd had a bit of green hair, but mostly gray or white or bald. And they weren't ashen and used up; they were stylish and healthy and dancing their hearts out.

So this is where the counterculture went when they grew up.

The next morning, I phoned my landlady and asked if she'd be willing to extend my lease on a month-by-month basis.

Chapter 7

Sensual Desires

People disagree about the year of Maharishi's birth, but everybody knows the day—January 12th. When Melinda gave me my ID card, she told me that it would get me into the Golden Dome for the biggest holiday celebration in the Movement's calendar.

I pulled into the dome's parking lot on a cold and drizzly afternoon. A crowd of people—many families with children, along with teenagers and middle-aged singles—converged on the dome from all directions in cars and on foot.

As you get closer, the spiritual center of Maharishi's Movement begins to show its age. The gold roofing material is faded and blotchy. Pieces here and there seem to be missing, although that may be a result of the reconstruction.

Put up in a hurry around the time of the Taste of Utopia course in the early eighties, the dome violates many of the Vedic building codes that Maharishi started to enforce later on. It's round instead of square. The original entrance faced west, the direction of "poverty and lack of creativity." (According to rumor, when asked why the dome was built facing the wrong way, Maharishi replied, "I didn't know.")

Until the dome can be retrofitted to block out evil, people enter the lower level through the back door by the parking lot.

I followed a woman and her two kids into a dim, dreary corridor. The concrete walls were stained and damp. The throw rugs on the concrete floor were soaked and muddy. The place was a good reminder of the unity between the spiritual and the material—upstairs, the world's most highly evolved beings rise off the ground in ecstasy, while down here the concrete weeps and the mold spores blacken. It's heaven's mud room, the steam tunnels under the City of God.

The corridor opened onto a cavernous shoe room crammed with large wooden racks populated floor to ceiling by wet and muddy footgear. I slipped off my loafers and left them in what I vainly hoped would be an obvious location on a shelf next to the men's room.

A group of young girls in the green plaid dresses of the Maharishi School of the Age of Enlightenment emerged from the ladies' room and ran up the Grand Hotel–style curving staircase that led up to the meditation hall. I followed them into a domed lobby where people were mingling before entering the main dome.

The people here looked like Movement regulars—thin men in light suits and trim ladies in ankle-length dresses. I was pleased that nobody seemed to take notice of me. However, at the top of the stairs, I saw the checkpoint where security men examined the badges of people entering the dome.

The bouncer for the Golden Dome of Pure Knowledge was no ninety-pound bliss ninny in a gold tie—he looked substantial enough to provide a real threat. I held up my badge as I approached him, but he barely glanced at me. I just sashayed by as if I were one of the regulars who came in to hover in the air every morning before breakfast.

Movement security sure has come a long way from the time when there was one guy who sometimes checked your meal pass when you entered the dining hall and sometimes didn't bother. What were they guarding us from? Demons? Christian fundamentalists? Gate crashers who want to levitate without paying their dues?

I walked into the dome and quickly realized what all the fuss was about. Anyone would recognize it as a holy place. Although the building is comparatively recent, it has the deep stillness of an old cathedral after centuries of prayer. The muted sunlight from a window at the peak of the dome softened the room's few edges into a single, womblike space the size of an aircraft hanger. Hundreds of people could fly around in here without bumping into each other.

For the birthday celebration, however, everybody was earthbound. There were people throughout the dome sitting cross-legged in ones and twos and small groups on the foam mats that covered the floor of the hall from one end to another. The rumpled sheets on the foam made the dome floor look like a huge unmade bed.

I climbed onto the foam and my foot sank down as if I were walking on new snow. The floor was covered with the belongings of dome regulars—pillows, water bottles, sweatshirts. It was like a giant slumber party.

I passed a guy sprawled out on the foam covered in blankets head to foot. He ignored me. All the people entering the dome walked by in silence or chatted quietly between themselves without giving me as much as a glance. There didn't seem to be any order or protocol; people just walked in and sat where they pleased.

I staked out a piece of foam not too far from the front entrance and sat down cross-legged. People continued to file in quietly, and most took seats closer to the front of the dome, where a huge projection TV screen displayed the words "video feed" over a dark blue background.

A group of college-age kids came in talking a bit louder than the rest. One of them—a largish girl in very loose-fitting slacks and blouse—bounded across the foam as if she were an astronaut enjoying zero gravity. They would have fit in well at any undergrad campus.

"Jai Guru Dev," said a woman in a white dress, standing under the video screen. "Welcome to the replay of the January 12th celebration. The program lasts for about four and a half hours and Maharishi speaks for about three hours."

The huge screen flickered and cleared to reveal two Indian priests in mid-chant. One was young and one was middle-aged. Both had light brown skin, black hair, and orange robes. They chanted from memory, staring straight ahead into the camera.

I don't know about the magical properties of Vedic sounds, but the chanting does have a nice soothing effect. The Sanskrit words flow by in staccato beats, gently rising and falling, seemingly without end. Like sitar music, it's pleasantly hypnotic even if you don't understand what's going on.

The Indian pundits chanted on and on as more people entered the dome and found seats. Most people kept silent out of respect for the Vedic recitation, although I heard a small buzz coming from the rear of the building. I turned around and saw the group of kids I'd noticed earlier, standing and lounging in a knot, talking and laughing in a polite and well-behaved but still juvenile way. It was like a family gathering for Thanksgiving dinner.

After twenty minutes of chanting, the Vedic warm-up team closed with a final "ommmm," and the camera switched to Maharishi. The tiny guru—now almost completely bald with a few wisps of white hair—sat motionless on a white couch surrounded by voluptuous bouquets and garlands. His eyes were closed and he seemed lost in the silent depths of bliss consciousness. After several minutes, his lips moved. "Jai Guru Dev." Then he began to sing in the faint, cracking voice of a man who had just returned to his body after a long immersion in the Absolute. Each syllable of the Sanskrit hymn hung in the air of the silent dome.

The man sitting on the foam next to me stood up and bowed his head. Others stood and picked up the faint chant. It was the Holy Tradition— the invocation of the ancient masters that every TM teacher learns and recites for each new student. Some of the people around me had their arms raised in supplication to the huge video image of Maharishi, as transported as fundamentalists at a meeting of the Promise Keepers.

I stood with my head bowed, trying to look inconspicuous, although it really wasn't necessary. Most people weren't chanting, and some remained seated or stretched out on the foam.

When the Holy Tradition ended, some people sat down and some fell to their knees and pressed their foreheads to the foam. This was way beyond anything I'd seen in the Movement. It reminded me of the stock answer we were supposed to give to non-meditators who inquired about the religious nature of the practice:

"TM is not a religion."

Finally, Maharishi opened his eyes and spoke.

"Today I have found the day to achieve that which all these half-a-century pursuits of my global Movement is achieving. Today I feel so fulfilled that the target has been achieved."

His voice grew stronger as he spoke. He talked for a while about the accomplishments of the Movement.

"It's a very great fulfillment for me to say that the climax of the blessings of our Vedic tradition of masters is at the dawn. . . . The first ray of the dawn, the first ray of the dawn, the first ray of the sun."

It's always been difficult for me to follow Maharishi's lengthy speeches. I'm stuck on the level of style and content, and what I hear seems vague and repetitive. That's not the point, of course. The point is *him,* being in his presence, getting his *darshan* (the blessing that comes from seeing a saint, even if it's just on video). Most Movement people understood this from the start, which is why they can listen in total absorption for hours. Me, I just get antsy.

It was more difficult back in the MIU classrooms with their hard-backed chairs and fluorescent lights. In the dome, however, it was easy to slip into the relaxed mood. People sat or stretched out on the foam and listened in the comfortable dim light, coming and going as they pleased.

I settled in as Maharishi's stream of consciousness took him from the Vedas to the state of higher education to war profiteering and the perfidy of scientific journals that refuse to publish the Movement's research studies for fear of upsetting their clients in the weapons industry. At one point, Maharishi announced that he had assembled the "greatest scientists" of all time. At this, the camera cut to a lineup of stone-faced men in off-white suits.

"British! Germans! Americans!"

That brought me back into focus. Maharishi was admonishing the governments of the world.

"They say they have no money."

He mentioned various systems of government—"democracy, communism, dictatorship"—and belittled the differences as "children playing with sand on the beach."

"NATO should wind up. It should wind up. And we'll see that it's winding up. Because darkness winds up with each ray of the rising sun, the rising sun, the rising sun."

It was a side of Maharishi that I'd never seen before—angry, bitter, judgmental. I'd heard rumors about his temper, however. Some people in the Movement claim that Maharishi's tantrums and other odd behaviors are subtle parts of his teaching. They're supposed to shake us out of the expectations and attachments that keep us from enlightenment. If so, I can't tell the difference between his subtle teaching methods and plain old grumpiness.

"British! Germans! Americans!"

He damned them again and ordered them to "get out and make way." Conspiratorial laughter echoed through the dome.

Maharishi went on and on as most of the dome crowd relaxed on the foam, enjoying a break from their jobs or classes. A guy near me was propped up on pillows and lightly snoring. I noticed a young man and woman happily curled up in each other's arms, apparently oblivious to the cosmic events surrounding them. Nobody seemed to care as long as they didn't make noise. I liked the atmosphere of casual belonging. It felt comfy.

After a couple of hours, my back and fanny were getting tired of the foam and my mind was getting tired of Maharishi. I stood up, wobbled a bit on the foam, and walked toward the door.

On my way to meet Doug at Revelations, I drove past the university. Construction barriers and ribbons of yellow tape marked the latest demolition sites. Most of the buildings on the old quad were gone. The chapel was still standing, lonely but dignified, waiting to meet its fate.

I walked into Revelations and found my friend sitting at a table with an espresso and a copy of *Rolling Stone*. He was eyeing an attractive, gray blond–haired woman at the next table. I got a mug of coffee and joined him.

"So are you dating anyone?" I asked.

"Nah. The girlfriend thing never works out." He said it in a flat, matter-of-fact way.

"There was a joke going around maybe twenty years ago," he continued. "A computer program predicted that in ten years, everybody in Fairfield would have been married to everybody else in Fairfield."

I chuckled. The Movement community was a romantic soap opera even back in my day.

"Then they updated the joke: A computer program predicted that in ten years, everybody in Fairfield would have taken a training seminar from everybody else in Fairfield."

We both laughed. This part of the story was new to me, but I'd seen enough posters around town to get the drift.

"Everything passes through here sooner or later," he said. "We've had channelers, men's groups, women's groups, pyramid marketing."

"So the Movement has competition?"

"Yeah. It's still the biggest spiritual attraction in town, but a lot of people moved on. They got fed up with the high prices or the heavy-handed stuff, or they just wanted something new. It's wide open now. Did you hear about Robin Carlson?"

I said I hadn't.

"He started out in the Movement, but something happened to him and he decided that he was a great enlightened master. So he went out on his own and started building his own group. He had a ceremony down at Waterworks Park, where he proclaimed himself the Shankaracharya of the Western Hemisphere. Or maybe it was just North America. I don't remember."

I shook my head. Shankaracharya was the official title of Maharishi's master, Guru Dev. As such, he was a successor of Shankara, one of the most important figures in Indian religious history. For a Movement guy to set himself up as a Shankaracharya would be like a parish priest calling himself the Pope.

"He printed up a bunch of flyers promoting himself and he rented a helicopter. One day, when everybody was meditating in the dome, the helicopter flew over campus and dropped all the flyers. The campus security people went around and picked them all up. When everybody came out of the dome, there weren't any flyers left."

Doug grinned and took a bite of his sweet roll.

"So what are you into these days?" I asked.

"I still do TM. But I went to see Amma in San Francisco. She's got a pretty big following here."

Amma is Mata Amritanandamayi, an Indian spiritual leader known as the hugging saint. According to her Web site, "Amma comforts the hearts of thousands of people with her unconditional love."

"I saw her in this huge meeting hall. I got there pretty early, but there was already this big line that went through a bunch of rooms. I sat on the floor and meditated and every half hour or so I'd get up and move closer to the room where Amma was giving out hugs. The crowd kind of narrows down into a funnel as you get closer, and there are these Indian guys who guide you to her. She hugged me and rocked me in her arms and I broke down and cried."

He gave me a hesitant look, as if the story of his hug might not go over well with another guy. At first I thought it sounded kind of lame. But then I realized: Maharishi was never big on personal relationships with his admirers. He was chilly and intellectual and then he was gone, isolated behind the walls of his compound in the Netherlands, a recluse accessible only to the members of the inner circle. For the Movement's rank-and-file, starved for personal contact, the idea of a guru who hugs people would be a revolution.

"They say that in India Amma hugs thousands of people a day. She actually gives money to the poor!" This idea was so outrageous that Doug leaned over and bugged his eyes at me.

"By the way," he said after he'd drained his espresso, "I phoned Jamie last night. I told him you were here and I said you were looking for Beth." I perked up. "He gave me her address and phone number."

This is Beth. Please leave me a message."

"Beth, hello!" I tried to sound enthusiastic, but not nervous. "It's great to hear you."

I urged her to call, left my number, and hung up thinking how small her voice sounded. The piece of paper next to the phone had her number in Doug's handwriting along with an address in Louisville, Kentucky, the city she grew up in.

Beth always had a bit of southern belle to her. Back in the seventies, half of the men on campus were in love with her. She dated Ron for a while, and Jamie off and on.

I recalled the winter night that she showed up at my door in tears after a nasty spat with her current boyfriend. She told me I was a good listener, and I listened a lot. By spring, we were best friends. Then we were lovers.

It's not that sex—like beer or marijuana—was totally unknown at Maharishi International University. There certainly weren't any written rules against it. However, Maharishi made it clear that celibacy is the quickest path to enlightenment. (According to his biography, when Maharishi learned that the Beatles accused him of seducing a female follower, he exclaimed, "I don't know anything about sensual desires!") Sensual desires are one of those things that you just don't do, and those who *do* do them, well, they do so in secret.

Given the general chastity of the place, and our previously platonic relationship, I think our first kiss surprised both of us. Beth and I were walking through the old campus under the moonlight when she steered me off the sidewalk and pointed to a ring of mushrooms sheltered in a small grove of trees.

"There's a fairy castle in there," she said. I thought about it for a second—yes, pixies of the storybook sort would choose just such a place to build their home—and then I slid my arm around Beth's waist. She responded immediately, turning to me and pressing the full length of her body to mine. Our mouths fell together in delight. When we broke for air, we looked around and realized that we were standing in plain view, where anybody could see us disregarding Maharishi's instructions about the evolution of consciousness. We stepped into the grove of trees where it was dark and the fairies didn't mind our sensual desires.

The next evening, Beth invited me to her room to watch TV. That was another activity that came in low on the evolutionary scale, so she usually kept the volume down when she indulged.

Beth met me at the door of her room wearing an embroidered red and yellow silk robe. "You'll love this show," she said as she knelt on the floor, reached under her bed, and pulled out her little Sony TV. "It's *wonderful!*" She stood for a moment looking around, trying to figure out how two people could watch television in a room barely large enough to sleep one.

"Do you mind sitting on the floor?" she asked. I said it was fine. She placed the TV on her narrow bed, plugged it in, and pulled out the rabbit ear antennas. We sat on the floor facing the tiny screen. It was a cool evening. Beth unfolded a quilt and we pulled it around ourselves and huddled together.

She turned on the TV and we watched the opening credits of *Starsky and Hutch.* Two buddy cops—one blonde, one brunette—drove around in their red Camaro chasing bad guys while funky electric guitars blasted their theme song. Beth turned down the volume.

"My neighbors get mad at me," she said. The walls of the prefab dorm—thrown up quickly during the draft deferment boom of Parsons College—were as thin as cardboard. Beth lowered the volume to a point where she figured that nobody else could hear it, but then we couldn't hear it, either.

"I usually listen with the earphone," she said, dangling it between her fingers. I took it and told her I had an idea. I plugged it in, took off my glasses, and wrapped the wire around the left bow a couple of times. Then I put my glasses back on and pulled Beth close to me and we placed our heads together with the earphone dangling between my ear and hers. It produced enough volume to follow the plot.

Starsky—or Hutch, I can't remember which—was kidnapped by the mob. They tied him to a chair and, every few hours, injected him with heroin. The poor guy was a brainwashed zombie by the second commercial break.

Outside in the dorm's common area we heard doors opening and people talking and feet milling around. Instinctively, Beth turned down the volume even further.

"If you'll all please take a seat," said a blissful female voice just outside Beth's door. "Welcome to the Wednesday evening meeting. We'll begin with a beautiful tape of Maharishi's latest knowledge."

"Oh no!" Beth whispered in a barely audible voice. "I forgot it was tonight."

MIU students were supposed to devote a chunk of their extracurricular time to the Movement. One plan was to divide the student body into teams that would travel across the Midwest spreading the word of Transcendental Meditation. Everybody on campus was automatically a member of the group, and attendance at meetings was supposed to be mandatory.

Beth and I kept as quiet as possible. I think we both were waiting for the inevitable knock on the door.

The tape started and I heard Maharishi's squeaky voice lecturing about the infinite unbounded nature of consciousness and its spontaneous and effortless manifestation in the field of relativity.

On screen, Hutch, or Starsky, was desperately searching for his drug-addled partner.

Outside, we heard Maharishi talk about the natural tendency of the mind to seek subtler and subtler levels of awareness until it arrives in the blissful field of pure consciousness.

I felt Beth's warm breath on my cheek. Under the quilt, I moved my hand silently across her thigh, following the embroidery on her robe across her curving hip, up her waist, and onto her breast.

She inhaled audibly. It was very loud. My fingers traced the embroidery across her nipple, which rose under the cloth.

She gasped as Maharishi made an analogy between the clear sap flowing through the stem of the rose to make this petal red and that petal red and the pure, unbounded Absolute which flows into the Relative and gives rise to all the diverse qualities of this and that and this and that . . .

We were both breathing deeply and trying to keep it as quiet as possible. It wasn't easy, but we managed to lean back on the floor and loosen our clothing without making any noise. We wrapped our arms and legs around each other, enclosed in a sweaty cocoon of embroidered silk and quilt and clothing with a thin wire coming out of one end and running across the floor up to the TV on the bed where Starsky, or Hutch, was preparing to rescue his partner.

Maharishi said that the nature of life is bliss, bliss, blisss . . .

"Oh . . . oh . . . oh . . ."

Beth whimpered softly. Pleasure ran up my spine and flooded my brain. A SWAT team burst into the underground mob hideout and Starsky and Hutch were reunited in a tearful embrace. Beth and I exhaled and rolled apart.

The dreaded knock never came.

We carried on like that, trysting in the shadows like ninjas, for the better part of a year. I was enraptured, and Beth was happy, too, although she would occasionally say something like "We really shouldn't be doing this."

Her big heart made Beth distractible by love and sex, but down deep she was the real thing—she wanted Cosmic Consciousness more than anything else. As I got to know her better, I realized it went further than that. She wanted the other world more than this one.

"It's all possible," she explained to me one evening. "Materialization, immortality, mind-melding. People around Maharishi are starting to levitate."

I smiled weakly. Beth was starting to catch on to my thick-headed disinterest in miracles. She gave me a knowing stare.

"Imagine making love purely on the level of consciousness," she said. "You're in a physical body now and all you can do is penetrate another body. But think about what you could do in a body of pure light and energy."

It was hopeless. Beth gave in and patted my arm gently with a condescending grin. "It's okay, you'll understand," she said. She could afford to be patient for a little while longer. After all, the Age of Enlightenment would arrive any day.

Chapter 8

Fairfield Life

D o you have anything about the Maharishi Effect?" I asked the MUM librarian.

"That would be in the Science of Creative Intelligence collection." He led me behind the circulation desk and unfastened the velvet rope that protected the Movement archives. "You can come in," he said.

I walked into a canyon of shelves containing what looked to be every word written by or about Maharishi and Transcendental Meditation.

"Is there any particular aspect of the Maharishi Effect that interests you?" he asked.

"Scientific research?" I said.

He pulled a paperback with worn covers from the shelves and handed it to me.

An investigation into field effects of consciousness from the perspectives of Maharishi's Vedic Science and physics.

By . . . oh goodness!

I had a brief flash of Kurt Kleinschnitz sitting in a classroom a few seats down from me during one of the many tape-recorded lectures by Maharishi. He wore a three-piece suit and a profoundly serious expression. As I did my best to stay awake, he was furiously writing word-for-word notes and triple-underlining significant points.

Now here he was, decades later, a Ph.D. physicist specializing in the Maharishi Effect. As the librarian pored over the stacks, I opened Kurt's book.

"The Maharishi Effect is the phenomenon of improved societal trends resulting from the practice of the Transcendental Meditation program or group practice of the TM-Sidhi program by a small fraction of a population. The Maharishi Effect is fundamentally a phenomenon of radiation of evolutionary influence arising from the enlivenment of pure consciousness . . ."

The librarian handed me several more books, including a couple with gilded pages. I carried them to a chair next to a droopy potted palm that might have occupied the same spot in my student days.

Some of the books were light PR and some were hard science, or gave the appearance of hard science. Kurt's was the most densely technical. I flipped the pages and paused at a table of numbers—raw EEG data—so small and tightly packed that the page was almost black.

Kurt is one of many Movement scientists to study the brain waves of people practicing TM and, more recently, the TM-Sidhi program. His book describes additional effects that occur when a bunch of sidhas fly together. The consciousness of the person bouncing on the foam mat next to you somehow crosses the intervening air and boosts your own consciousness.

This is possible because consciousness isn't just an outgrowth of brain functions. It's a universal, all-pervasive "field" in the physical sense, like electromagnetism or gravity.

". . . the field of pure consciousness can carry an unseen influence from source to destination," wrote Kurt.

Two sidhas generate stronger consciousness than one, three more than two, and so on. Up to a certain point, the gains are mostly apparent to the people bouncing on the foam. Once the group size reaches a certain threshold, however, the effects radiate outside the meditation room hither and yon through the field of consciousness. People in the surrounding area, even non-meditators, experience the advantages—peace, harmony, fewer traffic accidents, lower inflation rates, etcetera.

The critical number is the square root of 1 percent of the surrounding population. For instance, the population of my home state of Wisconsin is 5,472,299. One percent of that is 54,722, of which the square root is 233. According to Maharishi's theory, then, a group of 233 sidhas practicing Yogic Flying together every day should be enough to eliminate or dramatically reduce crime, poverty, suicide, divorce, illness, accident, and unhappiness in every city and hamlet throughout the Cheese State.

Movement scientists claim that "nearly fifty research studies" prove the connection between Yogic Flying and the well-being of society. In a typical experiment, Movement scientists record the number of Yogic Flyers in an area, along with social statistics of some sort, such as the number of murders per day. Then they compare the Yogic Flying numbers to the murder numbers using a statistical technique known as "time series analysis." If they can show that the two series changed in sync over time (for example, the number of Yogic Flyers goes up on Wednesday and the number of murders goes down on Thursday), they can claim a cause and effect relationship.

As I skimmed Kurt's book, I had an odd sensation of nostalgia mixed with helplessness. It's the kind of book I used to pull off the shelf in my dad's laboratory on the Saturday mornings when he brought me to work with him. I'd stare at the numbers and elegant symbols without any understanding beyond a gut respect for the authority of science.

The more I read about the Maharishi Effect, the more uncomfortable I became. Cutting-edge physics or delusional bullshit, I had to know one way or the other, and I wasn't going to understand it without expert help.

In the MUM student union bookstore, I walked up and down past shelves filled with organic candy bars, parasols and purses with the school logo, many kinds of incense, party supplies, backjacks for meditation in the Golden Dome, and necklaces of red coral beads ("to cultivate the heart"), white coral beads ("to cultivate the mind"), and little brown *rudraksha* beads ("to cultivate celibacy").

In my day, a good half of the bookstore was occupied by actual books—textbooks and classics and current paperbacks from Thomas Pynchon to Carlos Castaneda. That was all gone except for a small display with a dozen or so classic novels. *The Red Badge of Courage. Ivanhoe.* Nothing controversial.

There was, however, a large display of Movement publications. One shelf had all of Maharishi's books—early titles like *Love and God* and *The Science of Being* and later ones like *Maharishi's Absolute Theory of Defense: Sovereignty in Invincibility.*

The science section had all five volumes of *Scientific Research on Maharishi's Transcendental Meditation* ("This is the research that is objectively documenting the dawning of Heaven on Earth").

A thick paperback caught my eye: *Human Physiology: Expression of Veda and the Vedic Literature* by Tony Nader, M.D., Ph.D. The pages were gilded with gold leaf and the cover price was $450!

I flipped through the book and stopped at a diagram of the human brain. It could have been a brain in any physiology textbook, with lines and captions denoting the various parts. The brain in this book, however, came with a map of the planets in the solar system. Lines connected the sun and the thalamus, the moon and the hypothalamus.

The name Tony Nader was new to me. I asked around and learned that he was Lebanese, a neuroscientist with a Ph.D. from MIT, and very much in Maharishi's favor. In recognition for his research into the connections between the Vedic hymns and the human nervous system, Maharishi gave Dr. Nader a unique reward.

A blue string hung out of a crack in the door of the MUM videotape library. I pulled the string and a bell clanged inside. The door swung open to reveal the tape librarian—a tall, skinny guy wearing a tie and glasses and a suspicious look. I smiled meekly.

"Hello," I said. "There's a tape I'd be interested in viewing."

"Yes?" he said, giving me a very serious once-over.

"It's the . . ." I felt silly even saying the name. "The weight-in-gold ceremony." He stared at me.

"It's on two cassettes," he said in a solemn tone. "Viewing it would take most of the afternoon." I imagined long hours of pundits chanting the Vedas interspersed with droning speeches by guys in cream-colored suits.

"Well, would it be possible for you to fast-forward it to the, um, the weight-in-gold part?"

He looked at me like this was the dumbest request he'd ever heard.

"We can try," he said. He directed me to the viewing area, a room down the hall with a bunch of televisions. I sat down and put on a pair of headphones as the screens around me lit up. The scene was the throne room/ TV studio in Maharishi's house in the Netherlands. His little bald head peeked out from under a warehouse load of flowers and gold ornaments.

Mercifully, the tape librarian fast-forwarded to the end of a speech by Dr. Bevan Morris—Chairman of the Council of Supreme Intelligence— who held forth from a podium next to his guru's throne. I caught a few of his last words.

"The supreme scientist of our time. Dr. Tony Nader, M.D., Ph.D."

A gold curtain parted to reveal the supreme scientist—a slender man with jet black hair in the regulation light-colored suit.

He approached Maharishi's throne with his palms pressed together and a garland of red flowers dangling from his wrists. The old guru accepted the flowers and Dr. Nader backed away, bowing and grinning.

Another skinny guy in a light suit—identified as Paul Potter by a subtitle on the video—took the podium.

"It is my honor, as Treasurer of the Maharishi Global Country of World Peace, to award Dr. Tony Nader his weight in gold."

The camera panned to show the fateful instrument—a giant scale, a balance of the sort held by statues of Justice. Its central tower was perhaps ten feet tall, draped in gold cloth, and surrounded by floral displays and baskets of fruit. A white crossbeam rested on a pivot at the tower's peak. Chains hanging from each end of the beam supported two circular platforms, one bearing a cushion for the posterior of the supreme scientist.

Dr. Nader, still grinning to beat the band, took his place on the scale, sitting cross-legged on one platform as the other dangled in the air. I noticed writing on the crossbeam above Nader, although the camera movement made it hard to read. It said something like:

HONORING THE DISCOVERY OF VEDA AND THE
VEDIC LITERATURE IN HUMAN PHYSIOLOGY

With the guest of honor in place on the scale, two cream-suited minions lifted a bar of gold bullion from a pile next to Maharishi's throne.

"This first bar of gold weighs twenty-five kilos," announced Treasurer Potter. Someone leaned over and whispered in his ear.

"12.5 kilos," said Treasurer Potter.

The two minions carried the gold to the scale and placed it on the dangling platform.

"Will this be enough gold?" asked Potter. The platform with its one golden bar hung in the air as Tony Nader grinned from his position on the floor. "No," said the Treasurer. "More gold is needed."

The minions placed another gold bar on the scale next to the first. The platform still didn't budge.

"More gold is needed."

Another bar.

"More gold is needed."

Finally, Tony Nader rose from the floor and hung in the air. He was still lower than the platform with the gold, however.

"More gold is needed."

This time, one of the minions placed a gold coin on the stack. Then another. Finally, the scientist and the bullion reached equilibrium as the two platforms hovered at the same level. Nader, swaying gently back and forth, beamed and pressed his palms together toward Maharishi.

Bevan Morris approached the suspended scientist and handed him a large book. I couldn't see the title, but I assumed it was a copy of Nader's magnum opus, *Human Physiology*. The book threw the scale out of balance and Nader's platform dipped.

"More gold is needed to balance the record of research," said Treasurer Potter. The minions applied gold coins until the two platforms once again hovered at the same level.

"And now," Treasurer Potter said, "to celebrate the weight in gold, I want to play my golden flute."

He did, raising the flute to his lips and playing a slow, mournful tune that sounded a bit like "The Battle Hymn of the Republic" rewritten as a funeral dirge.

When the golden flute music was over, Dr. Nader delivered his acceptance speech from his platform suspended several feet off the ground. He talked about his great discovery that the sounds of the Vedic hymns are encoded in the human body. He noted how the four sections of one of the Vedic books correspond to the four lobes of the brain. The planets are in there, too, as well as the sun and all the celestial bodies. And, of course, we owe this precious knowledge to Maharishi.

The tape went on, but I was already sinking into the stupor that accompanies all Movement speeches. I took off my headphones and looked around the room at the video monitors showing Tony Nader hanging in the air next to his golden reward.

I imagined Albert Einstein sitting on the giant balance getting his weight in gold for discovering the theory of relativity. No, it didn't work. Only in Maharishi's universe would the value of a person's scientific research be determined by how much they ate for breakfast.

The backyard of my apartment opened onto an embankment that sloped down to the track of the Burlington Northern Railroad. Every half hour or so, a train thundered by and rattled the windows and the glassware in the kitchen cabinets.

From my back porch, I could just see the edge of the park near the clock tower where a train derailed in the seventies. It happened in the wee hours and, by the time I got there the next morning, half of Jefferson County had turned out to view the wreckage.

The locomotive went off the track and took several cars with it. They were lying on their sides on the grass, hissing and steaming, a short distance from a row of houses that barely escaped destruction.

One of the derailed cars was a tanker filled with beer. The crash punctured the tank and a long stream of yellow liquid flowed from a hole in the car onto the ground.

There was an old farmer in the crowd, a grizzled guy dressed in overalls, staring at the derailed beer car and shaking his head in grief as if he'd lost a child.

"Alla that good beer," he said. "Watta goddamn shame."

Aside from the train's periodic noise and vibration, my back porch was a good place to hang out. I sat on a lawn chair with my laptop as dogs barked and babies cried and women hung laundry to dry in the sunshine.

I typed "Maharishi Effect" into Google. It gave me a ton of Web sites for Movement operations like MUM, the Natural Law Party, *Enlightenment Magazine,* the World Peace Endowment, and the Consciousness-Based Education Association. The site for the Natural Law Party of New Zealand was typical:

NEW ZEALAND'S ECONOMIC ADVANCE DUE TO MAHARISHI EFFECT

"New Zealand's spectacular advance in economic efficiency compared with other developed nations, beginning in 1993, was due not to government policies, but to the Maharishi Effect, a phenomenon in collective consciousness that was first identified 40 years ago by His Holiness Maharishi Mahesh Yogi."

Most of these sites recycled the same graphics and text—pictures of hopping sidhas, EEG charts of harmonious brain waves, and vague analogies with physics.

"Just as a radio transmitter can create waves in the electromagnetic field, individuals constantly create influences on all parts of creation simply because consciousness permeates every aspect of the material universe."[5]

There aren't a lot of independent Web sites on the Maharishi Effect or any other aspect of Maharishi's teachings. The few I located—like Trancenet and Suggestibility.org—are the work of disgruntled former roos who air the Movement's dirty laundry in all its glory.

Maharishi's corner of the Internet is cordoned off by a firewall—glowing testimonials on one side and scandalous accusations on the other. There isn't a whole lot in between.

The most interesting site I found is called Fairfield Life,[6] a meeting place where true believers and apostates discuss spirituality and the legacy of Maharishi's teaching. The range of viewpoints borders on the miraculous. For example, the following story comes from an anonymous poster who asked Maharishi ("MMY") to help him remain celibate:

"I came about three feet before MMY with some apprehension about his response. He . . . asked me, 'How long have you abstained?' I replied, 'Two years.' Then, firmly, 'But I need help.' MMY nodded, then closed his eyes, and went really deep into meditation. He surfaced about ten seconds later, and said, 'It is good.' Then MMY looked at me solidly.

"Then suddenly I felt a solid hard bolt of energy come from MMY and hit me between my eyes, which stunned me by the impact. Before I could figure it out, a second solid hard bolt of energy again hit me between my eyes. Then I noticed my seminal fluid rising up to the second chakra level. A very sharp pain began; it was like an icepick was slowly being pushed into me at the pelvic chakra area. It was very painful and lasted about 5 seconds. Then the rising fluid seemed to become transmuted into a dense vapor. . . . It was a very pleasurable experience. When it reached the level of my heart chakra, it paused and radiated outwards from my chest in all directions with a great feeling of splendor. . . .

"That was my initiation into celibacy. It was done by a mere glance from my MASTER. He put my physiology through a metamorphosis that to this day has not changed."

By contrast, here's an opinion from another Fairfield Life participant:

"Maharishi has always treated his students as children, with him as parent and absolute obedience a given. Almost everyone who attempted to grow up and make their own decisions about their own lives has either left the Movement or been drummed out of it.

"I think it's pretty simple. This is the only form of interpersonal relationship with which Maharishi is comfortable. He can't possibly change, so everyone is expected to conform to his limitations and stay a child forever. As someone said here recently, these are the only people he trusts with the future of the Movement. They have to have as little personality as possible and as little ability to stand on their own and make their own decisions as possible."

Reading the conversations on Fairfield Life made me curious about the person who started it. Moderator Rick Archer is a Fairfield resident who worked full-time for the TM Movement for twenty-five years.

"The highlight was being around Maharishi," he told me. "Being on courses with him, being on the international staff, going on trips with him, being in small meetings with him. I was absolutely in love with him and devoted to him. He has a completely charming and charismatic personality, a remarkable degree of darshan. He's just an extraordinary human being.

"I was never terribly unhappy in the Movement. There were times when I was, say, living in some small house with ten guys, having to put up posters in the rain. When I look back on it, there were many years when I was absolutely crazy. I got into an off-balance, bizarre, relatively dysfunctional state, at least compared to how I think and feel now. Maybe that was from too much meditating, but I suspect that it was more from a lack of critical thinking.

"I was on Purusha[7] for a long time. Generally, when you're on Purusha, you're willing to go anywhere and do anything that Maharishi wants. I did everything from operating a jackhammer to teaching in various contexts, going to the Philippines, going to India. You're expected to do whatever is needed.

"A fair number of Purusha get into the mentality that the world owes them a living because they're doing something so cosmic and valuable. I was like that—taking advantage of people, expecting them to support me financially. I cringe when I think about it now. I think it was very socially inappropriate.

"I think some guys are more naturally cut out for Purusha than others. There are some there who really have their act together and are quite sharp and dynamic fellows and others who probably wouldn't be able to function in the real world anyway.

"I wasn't terribly into worldly things, but I enjoyed them. I had my share of girlfriends before Purusha. But then Maharishi started making announcements that celibacy is more conducive to evolution, so I started doing that. Even when I was on Purusha, though, I had a long-distance relationship with a woman that I eventually married eleven years later."

I asked him how he thought that the Movement had changed over the years.

"Obviously the Movement has become a lot more elaborate and unusual. When I got into it we were teaching a simple technique and we didn't care what you ate or what you wore or anything else. We emphasized the point to people we initiated that we aren't going to give you any relative advice,[8] but people kept asking for relative advice. So eventually Maharishi, either out of the desire to help them or the desire to make money, rolled out one thing after another. Ayurveda. Vedic architecture.

"There's a guy who used to be in the inner circle, who was one of Maharishi's personal secretaries, who talks about how he saw the Movement change. Maharishi became more paranoid and suspicious of people. He began ostracizing people who might give him critical feedback and surrounded himself with yes-men. So there was this closed-feedback loop where there wasn't any real-world input. That's maybe why things got more and more strange.

"Maharishi always was very convinced that he wouldn't hire real-world consultants. He always felt that we know what's best. The people out in the world are ignorant and we don't really need their advice. We give them what we want and not what they want to hear. I've heard him say that explicitly, any number of times.

"Maharishi's always been into hierarchies, and more and more so over the years. The more important people and the less important people. The people with money and the people without money. He was always setting up structures and pecking orders. I think that's become more extreme and calcified over time."

I asked him for his opinion on one of the perennial questions in Fairfield Life and the wider Movement community. Is Maharishi in it for the money?

"I dunno, it's very puzzling. He lives in a nice comfortable house in Holland and he has everything he needs and wants, but he's not the kind of guy who's going to buy boats and fancy cars and go jet setting around the world. He works all the time and always has.

"I always assumed that when I was sitting with him in meetings, brainstorming until three a.m. about ways to raise money, that he sincerely wanted to save the world with that money. But when you see so much money raised, so many millions, and nothing much coming from it . . .

"You don't know. The people who would really have the inside scoop, they certainly wouldn't talk."

I asked him if there was a particular incident that led to his disenchantment with the Movement.

"It was kind of gradual. I got married in 1987 and we were both working for the Movement full time. I was on faculty at the university and I did various other things, but after a while there wasn't any position for me. I had to choose whether to stay on staff in some menial position or to leave campus. So after a lot of trauma, we moved into town and we kind of liked it.

"This was around '94. I was still going to the dome regularly, living in town, doing various computer-related jobs. For a couple of years, friends were telling me about Amma and how sweet it is to see her. I kind of wanted to and I kept bringing it up to my wife, but she said it was off the program and didn't want to do it. So finally in '99 we went to see Amma. We really loved the experience and we started going to see her regularly.

"Being Mister E-mail, I started notifying people of local Amma-related events like potluck dinners. I didn't think much about it, I was just using my regular e-mail address. But these notes got passed around and next thing I knew they called me up and said I'd better come in and see them."

Like many others before him, Rick was expelled from the Movement after straying too far from the fold. I asked him if he was bitter.

"It wasn't any big trauma; I tend to take things as they come. Some people who used to be close to Maharishi now think he's a total fraud. But in my case I can't jump to that conclusion. I take everything with a grain of salt and evaluate everything he says or does on its own merit. I don't assume, like a lot of people in the Movement do, that everything he does is divinely inspired and therefore infallible. I did assume that for a long time.

"I feel that everything in life is multifaceted, there is no black and white. The Movement, like everything else, is a mixed bag. There's plenty of good in there, and plenty of weird stuff, and perhaps the ratio has been shifting over the years. I don't dispute that my involvement, on the whole, was extraordinarily beneficial for me. It gave me a lifelong habit of meditation and spiritual seeking. I couldn't have asked for anything better."

Chapter 9

Supreme Political Science

O ne morning as I left Revelations after my morning coffee and muffin, I held the door for a stylishly dressed roo lady. She got into a BMW with a bumper sticker that said:

HAGELIN FOR PRESIDENT
NATURAL LAW PARTY

This was a big change. When I was in the Movement twenty-five years ago, politics was a no-no. One evening around the dinner table, I made the mistake of expressing mild support for the Equal Rights Amendment, and by God I might as well have dropped my pants, put on a pair of blue jeans, and announced that I was abandoning vegetarianism for a diet of human flesh. One patient soul took me aside and explained:

"Maharishi says that we shouldn't waste our time in the mud. We have a solution that transcends politics." In other words, the only way to change society for the better is to raise the consciousness of individual citizens, and the best way to do that is TM. Everything else—good works, group therapy, the League of Women Voters, philosophy, sainthood, Prozac—is second rate if not downright evil.

The Movement we knew kept its distance from politics and the rest of the world's institutions. There wasn't much advertising—just TM posters in store windows and word of mouth. The grassroots strategy worked great for a while, partly because of the Beatles and other free publicity, partly because Maharishi had the good fortune to be at the right place at the right time, and partly because Trancendental Meditation works.

I've never seen any hard data on the numbers of TM initiations. However, when I hear Movement people discuss the subject, the general consensus is that the number of initiations in the United States peaked in the mid-seventies and went downhill from there. Whatever else it might have been, TM was also a fad and, by the time that Ronald Reagan became president, the fad was winding down.

A lesser guru might have given up and returned to the Himalayas. But Maharishi never quits. If the people wouldn't come to TM, then TM would go to the people. Enlightenment would come from the top down, which meant compromise with the powers that be.

The Movement's biggest coup on American soil occurred in New Jersey in the mid-seventies. The New Jersey public school system instituted a pilot program for high school students to learn Transcendental Meditation. The Movement supplied course materials, including a textbook on the Science of Creative Intelligence, and initiators for the actual instruction, which occurred at the end of the semester off school property.

The result was a landmark lawsuit—*Malnak v. Yogi*—in which a coalition of parents and their supporters in religious and civil liberties groups sued Maharishi, the World Plan Executive Council, the New Jersey Board of Education, the state of New Jersey itself, and the United States Department of Health, Education, and Welfare for violating the establishment clause of the First Amendment. The judge agreed and struck TM from the Garden State public school curriculum.

In the years since then, *Malnak* has endured as a pillar of First Amendment law. It's been used as a precedent in a number of cases, including *McLean v. Arkansas Board of Education*, the 1982 decision that overturned a state law that ordered the teaching of "scientific creationism" in public school science classes.

After *Malnak,* Maharishi turned his attention elsewhere in the public sector. He took out full-page ads in high-profile magazines like *Janes Defence Weekly* to promote "Invincible Defense" through Yogic Flying. In 1988, he announced the discovery of "Supreme Political Science" for "problem-free government" and "conflict-free politics," also through Yogic Flying.

As far as I know, these and other campaigns never got much response from the U.S. Government. However, Maharishi did have one notable success overseas.

The Movement arrived in the Philippines in the mid-eighties. President Ferdinand Marcos, the country's supreme dictator, was nearing the end of his rope, suffering from kidney disease and public outrage at his corrupt and violent reign. As his hold on power trembled, the old despot kept up the illusion by staging huge pageants in his own honor. He commissioned his own Mount Rushmore, a gigantic likeness of himself on the side of a Philippine mountain.

Perhaps Marcos saw a kindred spirit in Maharishi. Perhaps he had one last glimmer of hope when he accepted the guru's offer of problem-free government through Yogic Flying.

We get the rest of the story from a Movement insider who was on the ground:

"There were some TM teachers in the Philippines trying to get things going there and I guess that they made contact with Marcos and there was some indication that he might be supportive, so Maharishi decided to blitz the place. So TM teachers from all over the world flew there and set up shop. Maharishi himself came there but it was very secretive, people weren't supposed to know he was there.

"We all went to the palace one day to honor President Marcos. We presented him with this big silver bell, the Bell of Invincibility. He gave a talk and everybody stood up cheering for him. It was all very bizarre because it was all scripted and, after all, the guy was a brutal dictator. We were standing up shouting 'Hail President Marcos' and it was like the crowds chanting 'Sieg Heil' to Hitler.

"The Movement tried to buy this university there and the whole populace freaked out. There were demonstrations in front of our hotel and banner headlines every day in the main newspapers. We were under lock and key in our hotel for over a month. We couldn't even go out on the streets. There were barricades and bomb threats. It was a wild scene. They just didn't want us coming in and taking over."

A photograph from a Movement newsletter of the period shows Marcos, identified as the "Founding Father of the Age of Enlightenment for the Philippines," looking emaciated and ill, standing next to the Bell of Invincibility. The caption notes that he rang his bell over and over.

Shortly after the Yogic Flyers started hopping, the Philippine military rebelled and the Founding Father fled his country in shame, ending decades of authoritarian rule.

After Marcos, Maharishi's most notable success was in Mozambique in the early nineties. The African nation was one of the world's economic basket cases when the Movement arrived there. They managed to convince President Joachim Chissano that TM would make his country "invincible." According to a September 2001 article in the British daily *Guardian*:

"The attractions of this to Mr. Chissano and his generals seemed clear. From the end of 1994, all military and police recruits were ordered to meditate for 20 minutes, twice a day. More than 16,000 soldiers were taught yogic flying and TM, according to Mozambique's defence minister. So were 30,000 Mozambicans, according to the Maharishi movement."[9]

Unlike Ferdinand Marcos, President Chissano was not one of the world's wealthiest men. Although desperately poor, Mozambique had a unique attraction to foreign interests. Decades of civil war had displaced countless people, destroyed vital records, and left the ownership of much of the country's land in question. This precarious situation—and the Movement's role in it—was described in a February 1994 *New York Times* article by Bill Keller:

"Since war-battered Mozambique began to look like a land of promise, it has become Africa's newest destination for prospectors of all sorts. Only one, though, has promised heaven on earth.

"He is the Maharishi Mahesh Yogi, guru of transcendental meditation, former spiritual adviser to the Beatles, and—according to the prospectus for his 'Heaven on Earth Development Project in Mozambique'—the would-be proprietor of a spiritual and ecological Utopia.

"In its full glory, the project envisions 49 million acres of land, one quarter of Mozambique, tilled by legions of Mozambicans whose inner harmonies have been recalibrated by meditation."[10]

Unlike the Philippines, there was no dramatic denouement in Mozambique. The military eventually put an end to compulsory TM instruction, although President Chissano continued to practice and endorse the technique. If the land deal was ever more than an agreement on paper, it probably ended when devastating floods inundated much of the country in the mid-nineties. In any case, the Movement doesn't seem to have a significant presence in the country these days. Perhaps cooler heads prevailed.

In 2002, Maharishi's representatives approached a tribe of indigenous Bribri in the remote mountains of Costa Rica. The Movement offered modern conveniences—satellite dishes for receiving the Maharishi Channel—and millions of dollars worth of the Movement's own currency, the Raam Mudra.

Three weeks after John Hagelin announced the historic agreement, President Abel Pacheco of Costa Rica expelled the Movement from his country. According to Security Minister Rogelio Ramos, "It was obvious that they were promoting an independent state within Costa Rica, and we can't tolerate that."

Maharishi's search for government funding was a huge undertaking on the order of the Manhattan Project or the quest for the Holy Grail. As far as I can tell, it accomplished very little.

I'm hardly privy to Maharishi's intimate thoughts, but, at some point, it must have occurred to him that the governments of the world weren't about to put up. It was time for Plan B.

The year was 1992, and John Hagelin was making his first bid for the Presidency of the United States as the candidate of the Natural Law Party. He sat in a TV studio facing Joe Namath, former pro-football great, long-time TM celebrity, and host of the Movement's first political infomercial. Hagelin talked about the problems facing the country and the innovative solutions that he would offer as President.

Hagelin's intelligence beamed through the TV. He's clear-eyed, articulate, knowledgeable, and very polished. He started with tons of raw IQ, but I'm sure he spent a lot of time honing his presentation, sort of like Michael Jackson practicing the moonwalk in front of his bedroom mirror, except with quantum mechanics.

Hagelin turned from the sleepy-eyed quarterback and directed his consciousness at the voters. He's telegenic with a sculpted white grin, boyish and professorial at the same time. When he talked about scientifically proven solutions to problems like crime and poverty, he modulated every word with practiced care.

Hagelin ran in earnest. In the presidential election, the NLP came in eighth, with 37,137 votes.

They tried again in 1996 and got 113,670 votes, coming in seventh, between the U.S. Taxpayers Party and the Workers World Party. The increase was enough for the NLP to bill itself as "America's fastest growing political party."

The Natural Law Party returned in 2000 and Hagelin gave it all he had. He appeared on C-SPAN, in the third-party debates alongside Ralph Nader and Pat Buchanan, in a full-page *Newsweek* feature, and on yard signs across Fairfield. His name was on the ballot in all fifty states, along with hundreds of fellow NLP candidates running for office at every level from the U.S. Senate to the local school board. Natural Law Parties appeared in Canada, England, Germany, Israel, and New Zealand. There was even a ladies' auxiliary—Mothers for Natural Law.

This time, Hagelin received 83,714 votes, down about 25 percent from the previous election. Not one NLP candidate—national, state, local, or international—won a race.

In a statement to party supporters, Maharishi said, "We were wasting our time in imaginary illusions of political sovereignty." He ordered his followers to pull the plug on the NLP. "Don't even waste time on closing it down," he said.

What if he'd won? At some point, Hagelin would have had to come clean and give a speech like this:

"My fellow Americans, as your President, I will ask Congress for funding to establish a group of 7,000 Yogic Flyers, who will ensure our national security through their daily levitations."

Anyone in the Movement can give you the basic details of the Maharishi Effect. Whenever I asked about the scientific research, however, I got the same answer: "You need to talk to John Hagelin."

Although he's no longer the standard-bearer of the Natural Law Party, Hagelin is still the head of the physics department at MUM. He's also the director of a Movement organization called the Institute of Science, Technology, and Public Policy. He spends much of his time on the road lecturing, speaking to the media, and meeting with various officials. It's probably fair to say that he's Maharishi's main spokesperson in the United States, if not the West as a whole.

With all of that on his plate, he's an elusive guy. A number of people told me that the best way to get in touch with him was through his press agent, Bob Roth.

That's how I met the Movement's North American Communications

Director. We talked over hot cocoa at Entrée, a comfortable little eatery just off the Fairfield square. He was telling me about San Quentin Prison when his cell phone rang.

"Hello, Bob Roth," he said. "Sure. You spell it M-A-H-A-R-I-S-H-I." He put the phone away. "That's what I do all day—talk with reporters. Now where was I?"

He was in the middle of a story from his early days as a TM teacher.

"I taught a TM class to inmates in San Quentin. To get into the inner part of the prison, you have to go through four gates, and at each one the person there tells you that if you're taken hostage, they will not negotiate for your life. The place was very stressful, very tense."

Bob speaks with a lot of animation. For a guy in his mid-fifties, he still has oodles of youthful enthusiasm.

"The interest in Transcendental Meditation among the inmates and staff was huge. And back then, no inmate would close his eyes anywhere— maybe in his cell at night to go to sleep—but not in the dining hall or any-place else.

"We had a group meditation in a room with forty inmates. You had the Mexican Mafia, the Black Panthers, the neo-Nazis . . . every radical, deadly group, but they all shared the common experience of drug addiction and ulcers and insomnia and high blood pressure. So they were drawn to learn to meditate.

"The supervisor—the chaplain—was a Baptist minister, and they were all meditators. We did this twenty-minute group meditation, and it was the deepest experience of Transcendental Meditation I have ever had in my life. I opened my eyes and looked around the room and saw a micro-cosm of the extreme ends of American society. All of them had this deeply restful experience and they all opened their eyes smiling. There's no BS in that situation. I realized anybody can do this—it doesn't matter what you believe in—anybody can meditate and benefit from it."

Bob's been meditating for thirty-five years. He became a TM initiator in 1972 and he's worked for the Movement full-time ever since.

I asked him about the Maharishi Effect.

"Well, this is just personal," he said. "I've seen the research. You look at it and you say, 'Okay, that could happen.' In 1978, there was a group of meditators in El Salvador. There were huge problems going on everywhere—the Middle East, Iran, Zimbabwe, Nicaragua—everything was exploding. I was invited to go down to El Salvador, which is right next to Nicaragua, to lead group meditation as a sort of buffer.

"So there were about seventy-five of us who went down. For two months, we were just going to meditate in this hotel. We'd been there about three weeks and there was a front-page article in the San Salvador newspaper saying that for the first time in about five years there had been no violent deaths in San Salvador in the three weeks that we'd been there. And there was another article that came out a little later wondering what the explanation was. It continued that way for the whole two months we were there.

"Now, I was raised skeptical. There's a side of me that accepted the whole intellectual, logical explanation for the thing . . . but I didn't know. That's why it was so dramatic—it was my own experience. It was like turning on a light in this violent city. The whole time we were there in El Salvador there was like one death when there had been hundreds. Then a few months after we left, I got a letter from someone there saying that it had started to creep back up again.

"This was a personal experience of 'Wow! This thing works!' Somehow, on a very fundamental level, when you meditate you wake up something—a level of unity, whatever—that connects us together."

When you hang with Bobby, as his friends call him, it's easy to get swept away. He could be putting his considerable skills and charisma to work at Microsoft and making a lot more money, but he's using them for a higher calling. The fact that a lot of people would scoff at his higher calling gives him unexpected dignity.

I told him that I'd like to learn more about the research on the Maharishi Effect. "Everybody tells me that John Hagelin is the person to talk to," I said.

"He's very busy, but I can get you some time with him."

—

Everybody tells me that you're the person to talk to about the Maharishi Effect."

"And right they are," said John Hagelin. I called him in his office in Washington, D.C., and began our conversation by asking how he got involved with TM research.

"I went from the Stanford University faculty, where I worked at the Stanford Linear Accelerator, to Maharishi International University in 1983. I wanted to participate in the new doctoral program in the neuroscience of human consciousness that was being established at MIU. I went to join this interdisciplinary exploration into the nature of human consciousness and the origins of human consciousness and the limits of human potential. I brought with me my National Science Foundation grant in the field of elementary particle physics and unified field theories. I was originally going to stay for a couple years, but I'm still there."

As he spoke, I pictured him as he appears in his video lectures—the erudite quantum physicist standing in front of a blackboard filled with equations, the supernaturally calm emissary of Maharishi, smiling into the camera and speaking in a voice that would soothe a mad elephant.

"To a casual observer," I said, "it might seem like a leap that you went from studying particle physics to research in human consciousness. At what point did you see the connection and at what point did you make the leap?"

"As a doctoral student of physics at Harvard, I began to see the connection once physics began to seriously explore the unified field. With the emergence of supergravity theory and subsequently the superstring, we really had viable theories of the unified field—theories that incorporate gravity and all the other forces and particles of nature and understood them as ripples on an unbounded ocean of existence.

"That started to connect with my own experience of inner unity and the Vedic understanding of unity at the basis of diversity. This was a convergence of two major traditions of knowledge—modern and ancient—

in a way that was very compelling and satisfactory to me. That convergence of the modern objective science with the ancient subjective science of consciousness was so important and ultimately has such practical significance to the world in terms of the Maharishi Effect, it became my principal focus of research."

"As I understand it," I said, "modern science generally views consciousness as an outgrowth of brain functioning. Yet your view seems the other way around. Can the two views be reconciled somehow?"

"The prevailing view of physical scientists is that consciousness is an emergent phenomenon of the electrical activity of the brain. There has never been any cogent argument to support that point of view and certainly no research to indicate that consciousness is created by the brain.

"Certainly the brain influences profoundly what we experience, but consciousness itself is not created any more than the unified field is created. The unified field is the abstract, non-material foundation of the material universe. The unified field is a field of intelligence, a field of consciousness. Universal consciousness is the foundation of matter and ultimately the foundation of the brain.

"For a century, philosophers have wrestled with this issue of subjective consciousness emerging from objective matter and have found it extremely problematic. Researchers in the field of psychology have tried to find that spot in the brain from which consciousness magically emerges, and have failed.

"The assumption that consciousness emerges from brain tissue is only an assumption—it's not founded in empirical fact. It is a natural assumption based on the bias in which physical scientists work. That bias comes from three centuries of investigation of dead matter.

"The physics of the last fifty years has overthrown that view. Quantum mechanics really topples that myth of materialism by revealing a wholly non-material reality at the basis of what we experience to be emergent matter.

"It's a picture that physicists have had trouble with. They can work the equations, but it's been difficult for physicists to come around in their understanding of the nature of consciousness, mainly because they are schooled in a tradition of classical physics.

"So, there are two understandings—the ancient, time-honored understanding of consciousness as fundamental, and this sort of modern understanding that consciousness is a purely superficial by-product of the electrical activity of the brain. That worldview is on the verge of obsolescence."

"Let me see if I have this straight," I said. "In your view, the unified field of quantum mechanics is conscious itself. And it's the same as, or somehow connected to, our individual human consciousness."

"The unified field is a non-material, self-interacting, self-aware, dynamic field of intelligence which is equivalent to saying that it's a field of universal consciousness. It has all the fundamental characteristics of consciousness.

"Human awareness can be trained to explore deeper levels of intelligence and consciousness during the transcending process of TM. In these more expanded states of awareness, the mind becomes subjectively unbounded. And that experience of unbounded awareness is the direct experience of this universal intelligence now being explored by modern theoretical physics.

"So it is a new understanding of consciousness as well as an ancient understanding, one that is corroborated by extensive scientific research, including research on the field effects of consciousness—or the Maharishi Effect. Those long-range effects of consciousness—the spreading of coherence and harmony in society through the group practice of TM and its advanced techniques, provides profound empirical evidence for consciousness as a universal phenomenon that extends far beyond the confines of a single skull."

"Let me play devil's advocate for a moment," I said. "I'm well aware of the feeling of unboundedness and oneness that comes from transcendence during TM. However, I could accept that those are subjective brain states. It seems like a leap to assume that there is some connection between those states within myself and a wider world. Are you saying that the best evidence for this connection is the research on the Maharishi Effect?"

"I would say that's the best evidence for someone who is not immersed in clear experience of unbounded awareness, the ability to move one's environment through an impulse of thought and experience fulfillment of one's desires.

"All the evidence suggests that human beings can move nature from within. If and when individuals start to float and fly, it would be a direct confirmation of the ability of human consciousness to function at the level of quantum gravity, and thereby escape the grip of classical gravity. It would be a striking confirmation . . . if and when we're ready to demonstrate such a thing.

"By the way, whether we demonstrate it or not, it's a very robust phenomenon in the history of human civilization. There's overwhelming evidence for the ability of the human physiology to fly or float or levitate. There are great saints in virtually every tradition of the world who have demonstrated levitation in public."

Throughout our conversation, I heard movement and muffled voices in the background. Hagelin occasionally broke off to confer with an assistant. When he did, I heard him speaking in the same deliberate, modulated tones he uses in his video lectures.

"As a layperson," I said, "I'm fascinated by the Maharishi Effect. But I'm intimidated by the technical nature of the research, the statistics, the jargon. Can you give me an overview in plain English?"

"The Maharishi Effect is the spillover effect of TM into one's social environment. The deep calm and deep peace which one feels during TM does have an inevitable spillover effect. No man is an island. Just as panic can spread through a room or an entire city, so can calm spread through the environment.

"Some of the ways in which we affect one another are pretty obvious and quite well known—a harsh word has a harsh effect on one's spouse. But there are deeper levels of human interaction that extend deep into the quantum mechanical level. These are inevitable, well-known mechanisms of long-range interaction."

I asked if he could give an example.

"Yes. None of them are terribly simple.

"Quantum mechanics highlights the interconnectedness of things. Let me explain an example of what's called quantum entanglement that will shed some light on the quantum mechanisms for the long-range communication and influences between people.

"Take a single particle, a pi meson. It has no orbital angular momentum. It doesn't spin, it just sits there. Now let it decay into two fragment particles, which are typically particles with spin.

"Since we began with zero spin, zero angular momentum, we know that those decay fragments must have zero angular momentum in total. So, if one is spinning 'up,' the other must be spinning 'down.' That's all common sense. It's perfectly classical.

"But quantum mechanics differs in the following way. Typically a particle, quantum mechanically, will not have spin 'up' or 'down' but some quantum coexistence of both. That's called quantum superposition, the simultaneous coexistence of incompatible classical realities.

"Now, what happens when you try to measure the spin of one of these decay particles? A classical measuring device can't measure both, just one or the other. If you ask 'Is this particle spinning up or down?' and perform a classical measurement, you will get up or down, not both. That result reduces the quantum coexistence of all possibilities to a specific, classical, concrete outcome. That's called the 'collapse of the wave function.'

"The amazing thing is what happens to the other particle fragment as you measure the first one. It also exists in a simultaneous coexistence of spin states, both up and down. However, it may have passed beyond the moon or it might be halfway across the universe.

"When you perform the measurement on the first particle and you discover that it has, say, spin up, the companion particle instantaneously collapses to a state of spin down."

Hagelin was leading me down a well-trod path. People who talk about the connection between consciousness and quantum mechanics usually come back to this example. It seems like a paradox—the experiment you do at one location apparently determines the outcome of events on the other side of the universe. What's more, the choices you make—do I measure a particle's spin or position or momentum?—seem to instantly propagate across the void as well.

This one niggling paradox, the famous "collapse of the wave function," launched enough books and videos to account for a good chunk of the New Age. Many people assume that the wave function proves that "you create your own reality," that human consciousness creates the physical world.

"This is the general quantum principle," Hagelin continued. "Any two systems—particles, people—that have been in a state of interaction, carry correlations with each other. Since the two fragment particles were once united in the original pi meson, they remain correlated forever. Those correlations exist between any objects that have been in contact—people, husbands and wives. When something happens to one of those objects, instantaneously, and across vast distances, changes occur to the other, correlated system.

"So the phenomenon of communicating information at a distance is well understood quantum mechanically. Individuals do have influences on other individuals that are on a subtler, quantum level of reality beyond the superficial forms of interaction with which we're familiar.

"We studied the effect on the Lebanon war of seven coherence-creating assemblies[11] over a two-year period. Each was large enough to have a predicted effect on the war. Each one produced an approximately 80 percent reduction in war deaths, war-related injuries, and a marked reduction in levels of conflict. That's counted by numbers of bombs dropped, bullets fired, and so forth. The results were highly statistically significant. Those are the sorts of really striking changes that were predicted in advance and studied and confirmed in this study."

Hagelin's assistant called him away briefly and I made a note to find out more about the collapse of the wave function. When he returned, he told me that he had a long list of people he needed to talk to. Before saying good-bye, I asked Hagelin why the Maharishi Effect isn't part of mainstream science and what could make it so.

"I would say that it is entrenched prejudice that extends to the scientific community. It would be nice if we were really living in a scientific age. We say we do, but in reality, scientific fact has only a limited effect on public policy, only a limited effect on the thinking of scientists. Everybody is very limited in what they will believe or what they can understand by their social roots and by their education. It's often said that it will take one generation of scientists to die off before a new level of understanding will emerge.

"We're trying to accelerate the process of scientific transformation."

Chapter 10

Bliss Ninnies

W hen I opened my apartment door, Sarah gave me a brief visual exam, perhaps to make sure I hadn't turned into a brainwashed cultist. Then she smiled (a bit relieved, I thought) and put her arms around me.

"Mmm . . . there's less of you," she said.

"I'm back up to three miles a day," I told her. I'd just returned from my daily run down B Street, the route that used to take Jamie and me past the farmhouses and the rock-throwing juvenile delinquents. Now it's lined with upscale Vedic houses that all face east.

We had dinner at Regina's, a restaurant that would have been good in Madison or Milwaukee or Chicago; in Fairfield, it was a certified miracle. Sarah nodded approvingly when I ordered tea instead of Guinness Stout.

"I've only been here three weeks," I said, "and I already have more energy and concentration. There's definitely something going on here. I don't think it's anything supernatural; maybe it's just how I react when I'm in this place. I don't even know if it's good for me in the long run. But I'm going to figure it out, and 'the only way out is through.'"

"So am I going to lose you to Maharishi?" Sarah asked. She didn't look worried, but I gave her hand a reassuring squeeze just the same.

"Probably not," I said. "My crap detector's too big. Besides, if I was going to go off the deep end, I don't think I'd do it over Maharishi. He still doesn't do much for me."

I thought of the people I'd reconnected with since I returned to Fairfield. They hadn't seen Maharishi since he retired to the Netherlands in the late eighties, but they talked as if he were just around the corner.

"A lot of people say something like, 'I knew the minute I saw him that there was nobody else like him.' They say, 'He changed my life forever' or 'I'd be dead now if it weren't for him.'

"One guy said, 'The first time I saw him I exploded into infinity.' They say they see light shining around him or that he answers their questions before they ask them.

"I just don't get it. He just doesn't do much for me. I've sat through hundreds of hours of his tapes and all I see is a little guy with a high-pitched voice who says the same things over and over.

"People tell me that it would be different if I spent time with him in person, but I doubt it. I'm just plain immune to charisma. It's a gift from God."

Sarah laughed and sipped her tea.

"Did I tell you about the one time I saw him in person?" I asked. She shook her head.

"Well, it was from a distance . . ."

During my sophomore year in college, Maharishi paid one of his only visits to the campus that bears his name. His presence had an odd transformative effect on everyone around me. They went from fairly normal college students to, literally, followers.

Everybody seemed to know where he was.

"He's at the Learning Center!"

"He's at the Chapel!"

"He's going to be in the Library in forty-five minutes!"

With each report, a mob swept across the campus in the direction of the sighting. Hundreds of men and women in their finest clothing swarmed this way and that like iron filings in a magnetic field.

I was walking from the student union to my dorm when I found myself heading upstream through a torrent of love-struck disciples.

"You're going the wrong way."

"Oh . . . thanks."

"You're going the wrong way."

"Uh . . . okay."

I slid into my building and closed the door behind me like a small-time pickpocket on the lam. After the ferocious crowd, the empty dorm seemed quiet and safe. I went into my room and sat down and opened a *Swamp Thing* comic book.

A rap at the door! Oh no! It's Maharishi and he knows I'm off the program reading *Swamp Thing*!

Fortunately, it was Doug.

"Are you hiding out from the bliss ninnies, too?" he asked.

"Yeah."

We got in Doug's beater car and drove to the Taco John's on Fairfield's west side. We sat in a booth for a good chunk of the afternoon, eating tacos and talking about the Sex Pistols.

As meditation time approached, we figured it was all clear back on campus. We drove to the parking lot across from the MIU library where Doug and I often meditated together in a couple of easy chairs in the reading room. Doug killed the engine and pulled the hand brake while I contemplated the grassy hill that sloped down from the parking lot to the library's front entrance.

Uh-oh . . . we blew it.

The library doors opened and disgorged dozens of three piece–suited men bearing flowers. They quickly lined up on both sides of the entrance, pressed their palms together, and bowed their heads. Maharishi emerged. As soon as he appeared, he stopped, raised his head, looked over his followers across the grassy hill, into the parking lot, through the windshield of Doug's car, and smack dab into my eyeballs.

Total . . . utter . . . silence.

Maharishi and I stared at each other for . . . what, three or four months? Then he turned and walked away and Doug and I exhaled loudly. It was the sort of dramatic experience that a lot of Movement people report having with Maharishi. It's part of his mystique and one reason why so many are drawn to him.

At the time, my prolonged eye contact with His Holiness certainly shook me up. But when it was over, I didn't feel transformed or any more attracted to Maharishi than I was before. It was just another strange experience of the sort that happens from time to time in the Movement.

I had another example during the campuswide assembly that evening. It was the highlight of Maharishi's brief visit, an address to the entire community in the old Parsons gym.

I arrived around dusk and joined the mob of people swarming around the basketball court. A brightly lit stage on one end of the court had floral displays the size of refrigerators surrounding a white-draped couch bearing the sacred deer hide that would protect our leader's posterior from any negative energy in the earth and its furniture.

I jostled through the crowd of thousands to the bleachers and walked up the rows of wooden boards to my seat. Eventually, everybody found their place and we all sat quietly facing the empty white throne. The old gym had no air-conditioning. It was very hot and close.

We waited. And waited. People talked softly, waited, stared at the brightly lit but empty throne, and waited some more.

The evening wore on. Maharishi finally emerged from a door near the stage flanked by a host of assistants and Movement luminaries. All noise ceased. Nobody applauded. Most people stopped breathing as they watched each step, each gesture, each nod of their leader as he passed.

Maharishi assumed the lotus position on his deer hide. He gathered the folds of his white robe about him and stared beatifically into the faces of his multitudes. Then we waited some more. Maharishi seemed content to just sit and stare. His lieutenants stood around talking among themselves for a while, then they sat down in a row of chairs next to the podium. One by one, they got up and took the microphone to tell the crowd what a momentous day it was and how fortunate we were.

It was getting very hot in the gym. Finally, the last of the second-stringers finished his spiel and we waited a bit longer as a sound tech adjusted the microphone in front of the white dais.

The hushed crowd waited as the sound guy worked. Not a whisper. Then, suddenly:

BRAAAAZZZZZZZPPP!

Some deadly circuit clicked in the PA system and the speakers emitted a horrible rasping crash. I jolted upright in my seat. On stage, the sound guy and the Movement bigwigs were twitching and gulping.

Maharishi didn't bat an eye. He just sat there as placid and motionless as always. The awful noise, which freaked out everybody else in the building, passed through him like air.

Finally, with the PA under control, the Founder addressed his faithful audience in a high, sing-song voice about the natural tendency of the mind to spontaneously and effortlessly seek subtler and subtler levels of awareness until it experiences the infinite unbounded field of consciousness . . .

It was very, very hot in the gym. I wanted to leave very, very badly. Could I just stand up and walk out? Everybody else in the place was staring in rapt awe at their guru, reverently soaking in every word. If I walked out I'd brand myself as a heretic forever. What on earth did they see and hear that I didn't?

I tried to pay attention one more time, but discomfort won. I stood up and sidestepped my way down the aisle past motionless bodies in suits and dresses. In a group of thousands, I was the only one standing and moving.

I stepped gingerly down the bleachers and walked along the edge of the basketball court feeling the weight of countless eyes on my back. I quickened my pace a tad as I approached the door. I pulled it open and took a breath of blessedly cool night air. Freedom at last.

The next day, the lead headline in the *Fairfield Ledger* was "The Founder Keeps Them Waiting."

Maharishi left as abruptly as he'd arrived and life on campus quickly returned to normal. Nobody commented on my early departure from the meeting. They were undoubtedly paying a lot more attention to His Holiness than me.

Late at night Sarah and I were lying in bed staring up at the candlelight flickering across the ceiling. The walls of my apartment were bare except for the large poster I'd tacked up across from the bed.

"Did you ever figure that out?" Sarah asked, pointing to the Constitution of the Universe. In the dark, the intricate patterns of Sanskrit hymns and mathematical equations congealed into a gray blob.

"Not really," I said. "At least not the details. But I think it's a table of correspondences."

Sarah said "Hmm" in a way that meant she didn't recognize the term. I reached over to the bookcase by the bed and pulled out a thick paperback I'd found in a used bookstore in Iowa City: *777 and Other Qabalistic Writings* by Aleister Crowley, the notorious bad boy of the occult. The candlelight was appropriate.

"It's like a spreadsheet for doing magic. The things in the rows and columns are supposed to be connected on some esoteric level. If you want to use magic to influence something, you look it up in the table and find the things that are magically connected to it.

"Say that you want to make somebody fall in love with you." I opened Crowley's book and thumbed through the pages of his immense table. "You could invoke Aphrodite," I said, pointing to her entry in a column labeled "Some Greek Gods." I moved my finger over the table to columns of perfumes and precious stones. "You could get her attention using sandalwood incense and turquoise.

"It's the same thing with the Movement stuff." I pointed to the Constitution of the Universe. "You use the Sanskrit mantras to influence these laws of quantum mechanics. It's like Hagelin said: 'human beings can move nature from within.' And Crowley defined magic as 'causing change to occur in conformity with will.'

"The Movement stuff looks more scientific than Crowley because of the math, but I think it's the same kind of occult reasoning. I don't know how you'd say for sure, but I think that what Maharishi is doing is as much magic as science."

"So . . ." Sarah said, a bit hesitantly, "is that what *you're* learning to do?"

I hadn't thought of it like that.

"I guess so," I said.

The weekend ended and Sarah drove back to Wisconsin. A feeling of deep loneliness grew in me as I watched her leave. I phoned Doug and asked him to meet me at Revelations.

"So, are you moving back here for good?" he asked as we sat down at our regular table.

"No," I said. "I'm just . . . trying to get my act together." Doug gave me an enthusiastic grin.

"Man," he said, "this is *the* place to get your act together. Everything you want is here. High tech. Organic living. Spirituality up the kazoo—every teaching in the world. And it's all really laid back!" He emphasized how laid back it was by waving his arms.

I was coming to understand that "every teaching" wasn't much of an exaggeration. It seemed like every church, sect, and guru—from tantric ecstatics to fundamentalist Protestants—had a seat at the table in Fairfield.

"It's funny," I said. "I was always the one who was skeptical about TM being the one true path, but I'm not really interested in doing anything else. I don't know why I kept up with it. I hit a plateau a long time ago. I don't feel like I'm any closer to enlightenment than I was back then; further away, maybe."

Doug nodded and we both stared at the floor for a minute.

"Remember when you and I and Jamie used to go running?" I asked my friend, who nodded at the happy memory. "That was the best I ever felt. Then I went and blew out my nervous system."

"Hey, a lot of people come back here after they burn out. A lot of them go out to the Raj for Ayurveda."

That was new to me, so Doug explained about Maharishi Ayurvedic Medicine. "It's the best thing in the Movement, after TM. Of course, I can't afford it."

Chapter 11

Perfect Health

T he Raj is "America's Premier Ayurvedic Health Center" and without question the ritziest spa in southern Iowa. Imagine one of the
grand hotels of yesteryear inexplicably teleported into the middle of the prairie. It was glowing in the sunrise as I approached it on a
long road lined with graceful trees.

I parked and walked through ornamental gardens into a white lobby
with a dark marble floor that reflected specks of light from the chandelier
overhead. Nice place—peach carpets, creamy upholstery, lots of gold and
marble. If Jay Gatsby wanted to purify his nervous system, this is where
he'd come.

"I have an appointment with Dr. Lonsdorf," I said to the quiet, efficient-
looking young man at the front desk. Dr. Nancy Lonsdorf was the medical director at the Raj. Like other physicians in Maharishi's health care
organization, she had an M.D. (from Johns Hopkins in her case) and
training in Ayurveda, the ancient Indian system of natural medicine.

"Down the hall to your left past the Herb Room," he said.

I walked down a long hallway of the partly institutional, partly swanky
kind I've seen in upscale private hospitals. It might have been a recovery
ward in Beverly Hills except for the paintings of Indian gods. There was a
pink Ganesh with his elephant head and a blue Shiva twirling his index

finger in a circle of flame. I stopped to study a painting of a monkey-headed deity labeled "Hanuman Holding a Mountain of Herbs."

"Are you Joof?"

I turned from Hanuman to see a severe-looking woman in a white lab coat.

"Yes."

"I am Gudrun," she said in a thick accent as we continued down the hall. "You will be seeing Dr. Lonsdorf and Professor Siddhu. They will both take your pulse."

She led me to a waiting room tastefully furnished in cream and powder blue and left me with a sheaf of papers to fill out. The first part was the usual doctor's office stuff: Any family history? Any artificial limbs? Any bad habits? That sort of thing.

The form got more interesting farther down. What is the consistency of your stool? (Circle one: hard/soft/loose.) What direction does the front of your house face? (Circle one: N/S/E/W.) What direction does the head of your bed face?

A fresh breeze swept over me.

"Geoff? I'm Nancy Lonsdorf."

I looked up at a slender, wistful-looking woman with light brown hair and a genuinely friendly smile. Dr. Lonsdorf is not just the most beautiful medical director I've ever seen, she's a walking commercial for Maharishi's health-care system. Her skin is flawless and her eyes alert and clear. She might be in her mid-forties, but it's impossible to tell. She'll look exactly the same when she's eighty.

"I see you've been meditating for almost thirty years," she commented, glancing at my questionnaire as we crossed the hall to her office. "How come you're not doing the sidhis?"

Before I could come up with an excuse, she motioned me into her office, which didn't look any more holistic than the clinic at my HMO. The most unusual feature of the room was a plump Indian gentleman in a white robe with an orange vest sitting at a little table in one corner.

"This is Professor Siddhu," she said.

The Professor pressed his palms together and made a slight bow of the head. "Jai Guru Dev," he said very softly.

"Jai Guru Dev," I said, making the same gesture as I sank into a chair by his table.

Dr. Lonsdorf pored over my form. "Some fatigue problems?" she said, glancing up at me.

"Yes." And trouble sleeping, digesting, concentrating, remembering, and getting it up. I checked the "fatigue" box because there wasn't any box labeled "Approaching fifty and rapidly falling apart."

Dr. Lonsdorf gave me a quizzical stare. I felt momentarily naked, as if she could see the doubt underneath my smile.

"How's your elimination?" she asked. "Are you regular?"

"Pretty much."

"Do you take any herbal medications or dietary supplements?"

"No."

"Well, we'll change *that,*" she said cheerfully as she got up from her desk and walked over to the little table by Professor Siddhu. "I'll take your pulse now."

Dr. Lonsdorf sat down beside me, took my wrist, and, with a demure smile, parted company with modern science.

In her book *A Woman's Best Medicine,* Dr. Lonsdorf describes the importance of the pulse in Ayurvedic medicine.

"The pulse is taken at the junction point between consciousness and matter, where a thought becomes a neurotransmitter, a biochemical, or a hormone. At that deep level, we can think of the pulse as an 'impulse' of awareness."[12]

In other words, your pulse is a direct pipeline into your thoughts and consciousness. According to Maharishi, consciousness is the source of the entire physical universe, including the human body. Any illnesses or other health problems you have originate in the depths of your consciousness. By tapping into your innermost essence via the pulse, an Ayurvedic physician can diagnose specific diseases with great accuracy and precision. Or so the story goes.

I couldn't see Dr. Lonsdorf's face as she leaned over my wrist, but I sensed her total concentration. She wasn't just counting heartbeats as a Western-style M.D. would; she was probing, exploring, tuning in. I imagined the rhythms of my consciousness beating within her.

"Ah," she said, looking up with a knowing smile. "Would you like a turn, Professor?"

Dr. Lonsdorf went back to her desk and began writing on my form while the Indian pundit took a crack at my pulse. He leaned over the table and engulfed me by the wrist as his American colleague had, pressing and releasing, drinking up my energy with all the information it contained. After just a few seconds, he released me and looked up with a placid expression.

"Hemorrhoids," he said.

Dr. Lonsdorf smiled. "See?" she said with a satisfied look. "He can get that specific."

Wait a minute . . . didn't I check the "hemorrhoids" line on the form?

She turned to the Professor and the two discussed my case at length in an Ayurvedic patois. It was hard to make out much, owing to the technical terminology and the Professor's thick accent.

"Pitta?"

"Yum," the Professor said, nodding.

"Prana," he said, which means breath or spirit.

"A sweet drink at noon?"

"Cardamom."

And so on. Dr. Lonsdorf scribbled busily all the while. Then, to me:

"Do you have any mental stress? Any anger? Depression?"

I nodded.

"This comes from an imbalance of Pitta dosha," she explained.

The doshas (there are three of them) are extremely important in Ayurveda. In the glossary of her book, Dr. Lonsdorf defines them as "the governing principles in nature." Her Movement colleague Dr. Hari Sharma says they're "among the first manifestations of consciousness into the realm of matter."[13]

According to Ayurvedic theory, the doshas combine to form every cell and organ in your body. They also regulate all bodily processes such as blood flow, temperature control, cell division, reproduction, and so forth. Each dosha has its own bailiwick. For example, Vata governs the nervous system, Kapha the muscles and skeleton, and Pitta—the dosha that's out of whack in my body—rules metabolism.

Of course, the doshas are unknown in Western scientific medicine. I was skeptical, but I was also doing my best to understand, so I nodded as Dr. Lonsdorf explained my condition.

"Your excess Pitta is like a fire in the midsection," she continued. She held her palms against her stomach to illustrate. "The heat from the Pitta rises up through the torso and into the head," she said, raising her hands along the path of my errant Pitta. "It collects in the head and causes various mental difficulties. Stress. Anger. Gray hair. Too much thinking.

"I'm prescribing a Pitta rejuvenation diet for you. It will help by cooling the heat from your Pitta imbalance. I'm also going to prescribe some Maharishi Ayurvedic products that you can purchase in the Herb Room." She turned to the Professor.

"How about Blissful Sleep?"

He nodded.

"Stress Free Mind?"

"Yum," he said.

Dr. Lonsdorf scribbled busily for a while, then handed me a stack of papers and handouts with guidelines and recipes for my new diet.

"I'm recommending that you stay on the rejuvenation diet for two months. You should feel a lot better by then. You've developed good consciousness by being regular in your meditation, but now your body is holding you back."

I thanked her and took my leave, saying one last Jai Guru Dev to the Professor as I backed out the door with my palms pressed together.

In Sanskrit, *veda* means knowledge and *ayur* means life, health, longevity, and vital energy. Ayurveda—the knowledge of life—is the old-

est system of medicine on the planet, in continuous use in India from ancient times to the present.

The old Ayurvedic doctors were way ahead of their time. For example,
a two-thousand-year-old Ayurvedic text contains detailed instructions
for a surgical procedure to remove cataracts from the eye. In addition to
surgery, the ancient texts contain a vast amount of practical information
about nutrition, exercise, disease, pharmacology, mental health, pedi-
atrics, and other medical topics.

Ayurveda's emphasis on prevention anticipated modern medicine by
millennia. If you consulted an Ayurvedic physician of the Gupta Empire
circa 400 AD, he would have encouraged you to eat a balanced diet, exercise, and get enough sleep.

In modern India, Ayurvedic practitioners and Western-style M.D.s exist side by side. Both are regulated by the government. Ayurvedic doctors
treat mainly the poor and the well-off who have exhausted all other av-
enues of hope.

Ayurveda was almost unknown in the United States until very recently. Today, however, it's one of the most popular forms of alternative
medicine in the country. Ayurveda took off thanks largely to Maharishi and the man who became the biggest Movement celebrity since the
Beatles.

Deepak Chopra, M.D., the phenomenally successful author and New
Age icon, rose to fame while he was a member of Maharishi's inner circle.
During his time in the Movement, he served as the director of Maharishi
Ayurveda Products International and he was an enthusiastic and articu-
late spokesman for TM. Many people assumed that he would succeed
Maharishi when the old guru finally "dropped the body."

Instead, the Movement lost one of its biggest stars when Chopra left
for a solo career in the 1990s. These days, Maharishi and Chopra run
their separate health-care industries alongside the many others who have
joined the field.

There may be a lot of Ayurvedic products on the shelves, but you can
always pick out Maharishi's by his picture on the label. The advertising is

also distinctive. I doubt that any health-care system in history ever made such extravagant claims. The ads for Maharishi Ayurveda offer the hope of "perfect health" and "instant relief for chronic disorders."

Then there's the matter of eternal life. According to one Movement Web site, "There is a very comprehensive way to move in the direction of perfect health and immortality: Maharishi's Vedic Approach to Health."[14]

W ell now, let's see what we've got here.

I opened the bag I brought back to my apartment from the Raj and took out several brown bottles with Maharishi's picture on the label. The snowy Himalayas framed the name of each product—Mind Plus, Blissful Sleep, Worry Free Tea, Stress Free Mind, and Elim-Tox-O.

The virtues were duly noted:

"Authentic formula."

"Increases mental energy."

"Over 5,000 years of clinical research."

"Verified by modern science."

Each label had a long list of herbal ingredients, including Indian Trumpet Flower, Winter Cherry, Spreading Hogweed, Muskroot, Heart-Leaved Moonseed, Clove, Butterfly Pea, Long Pepper, Licorice, Chinese Cinnamon, Giant Potato, and Yellow Berried Nightshade.

I opened the bottle of Mind Plus and took a whiff. It smelled like the Christmas fruitcake that sat in grandmother's cupboard since the Eisenhower administration. I was supposed to take two teaspoons of the stuff twice a day.

Might as well give it a try. I poured out a spoon of the dark, syrupy liquid and threw it back.

Yow! My glands contracted in terror. It tasted like fruitcake-flavored motor oil.

As the medicinal fruitcake vapor spread through my sinuses, I read a handout titled "Main Principles for This Balancing Diet."

"Food must be freshly prepared, preferably in your own home."

"Do not use frozen, canned, bottled, packaged, or processed foods."

"Do not consume any leftovers (i.e., food that has been cooked and then refrigerated)."

Uh-oh. This could be worse than I thought.

As I read on, I discovered an extensive list of food items that must be avoided if I want to cool my Pitta.

"No red meat. No oily or heavy food preparations such as fried foods, cream sauces, heavy desserts, or pies. No raw vegetables or salads. No potatoes, beets, or root vegetables (except carrots). No hot spices such as chilies, hot peppers, or jalapeños. No bread made with yeast, sourdough, or baking powder/soda. No pizza, cookies, chocolate, cocoa, candy, pastries, or baked goods. No curdled milk products such as yogurt, cheese, cottage cheese, or sour cream. No butter, cream, ice cream, or any other frozen desserts. No vinegar or vinegar-containing substances including catsup, mustard, pickles, olives, or relishes."

Etcetera. And to drink?

"No cold water or ice. No soft drinks or carbonated beverages or carbonated water. No alcohol. No caffeinated drinks (coffee, tea, or cola). No bottled, packaged, reconstituted, or canned fruit or vegetable juices."

Poor health was looking better and better.

I had to page through the document for a while before I could find a list of acceptable foods. These included:

"Plain, cooked tofu. Mung bean soup. Red, green, or brown lentils. Pumpkin seeds. Zucchini, fennel, cucumber. Unleavened crackers. Tortillas made without yeast or baking soda."

To wash down my unleavened crackers and cucumber, I could have "organic, non-homogenized milk brought to a boil and drunk warm." Alternatively, I could have something called *kanji,* for which the Raj thoughtfully provided a recipe:

"Cook a handful of rinsed cracked wheat or basmati rice in 3 quarts of water for 1 hour or more until it is very well cooked. Strain it and drink the liquid portion during the day between meals as often as you like."

The things a person will do for eternal life.

—

By the third day of my immortality diet I wanted to die.

A nice glass of iced tea would give life meaning again, but the diet banned any food or drink cooler than room temperature. No caffeine, either.

No baked goods—no bread or pizza or anything with yeast in it. Nothing uncooked—no salads or fresh fruit or deli stuff. Nothing oily. Nothing spicy.

What's the point of living forever if you have no reason to live?

Day 4 of diet. Get up. Think about coffee. Can't have coffee. Meditate. Think about toast. Can't have bread with yeast.

Report to kitchen for duty. Boil water for Worry Free Tea. Mix flour and water for tortillas. Roll out and fry. Boil milk. Enjoy delicious meal of boiled milk, tortillas, and Worry Free Tea. Think about coffee. Total time: 1 hour.

Drive to health food store and buy fresh zucchini and tofu for lunch. Steam zucchini, boil brown basmati rice, sauté tofu with Maharishi Pitta Cooling Seasoning Mixture. Enjoy. Total time: 2.5 hours.

Try to get something done.

Simmer brown lentils. Serve over more brown basmati rice. Force down last of godawful kanji. Flush leftovers down garbage disposal. Total time: 1.5 hours.

Go to bed frustrated, pissed off, and thinking of coffee.

Day 5. The instructions for my diet have a section called "Subjective Experiences."

"In the first week, you may not feel better yet, and in fact you may feel some fatigue, transient digestive symptoms, or moodiness as impurities and wastes begin to be eliminated from your system."

Moody? Just because I spent my entire day in the kitchen and lived on lukewarm rice water? Just because I had a pounding headache and my arms and legs hurt?

What I wanted more than anything was something cold to drink. Ice water, soda, juice . . . anything. And I wanted to eat something that crunched when I bit into it instead of slithering past my gums without putting up any resistance.

Most of all, I wanted my life back.

Dr. Lonsdorf defines the doshas as "the governing principles in nature." Okay . . . but what *are* they? Her book offers the following explanation:

"The five Ayurvedic *mahabhutas* or elements from which we are created are known as earth, water, fire, air, and space. . . . From these five mahabhutas arise the three doshas . . ."

The five-element theory used to be state-of-the-art physics. Aristotle wrote about it in the fourth century BC, about the time that Ayurveda was beginning in India. It was still mainstream science in the Renaissance when alchemists tried to produce gold by rearranging the fire and air inside of lead.

Western science moved on and now recognizes 116 elements. Ayurveda still has the same five it always had.

Most days, I don't care how many elements there are. But we're talking medicine here. If I'm sick, I want a treatment that comes with solid explanations. My doctor can explain an X-ray down to the level of Biology 101; when Maharishi's Ayurvedic doctors try to explain the doshas, they have nowhere to go except fire and air. No escape from the endless loop of defining one supernatural thing in terms of another. No standards except faith for believing in five elements instead of four or twelve or a thousand.

A dog barked.

It was getting too dark to read. I looked up from Dr. Lonsdorf's book and set it down on the floor of the little porch in back of my apartment.

As the shadows deepened, I thought about the pills I was taking—
Mind Plus and Blissful Sleep and so on.

Sarah wouldn't want me to swallow this stuff on faith. Maybe it was
foolish, but I remembered how good I felt back when I was on the path.
That clear-headed feeling of serenity was all I cared about. I wanted it
back, and if getting it meant taking pills made of fire and space . . . well,
maybe I'm not as skeptical as I thought.

Maybe Fairfield was where I belonged.

Day 10. I've eaten food my whole life, and I've worked a bunch of jobs,
and, let me tell you, this diet resembled full-time employment more than
eating. For example:

The one exception to the diet's embargo on curdled milk products was
a yogurt drink called lassi. Here's the recipe from the Raj:

- 3 parts water (room temperature)
- 1 part yogurt
- Sugar
- Rose water
- Fresh cardamom powder

Fine so far. Oh . . . wait, there's some fine print:

"Lassi should be made from homemade yogurt made the night before
and not refrigerated."

Good grief! Maharishi expected me to make a quarter cup of yogurt
every night! If I made any more, I'd have to find somebody else who was
willing to eat it or throw it away.

This must be how they did things in India two thousand years ago before the evolution of convenience. The woman of the house drove the ox
cart to the market every morning to buy what she needed that day. Then
she made the bread and yogurt and fed the family and if there was any-

thing left she pitched it before it went rancid in the boiling sun. Total freshness; no convenience.

From my experience living a two-thousand-year-old lifestyle, Ayurvedic food prep takes about five hours a day. The time wouldn't be a problem if everybody agreed with Maharishi's views on gender (women stay at home to cook and raise children). They don't even do that in the Movement, however. In the real world, the Ayurvedic lifestyle has a long way to go before it competes with Burger King.

That's a shame, because my new diet was way healthier than the quick sludge I used to eat.

What's more, it seemed to be working.

Chapter 12

The Brain Integration
Report Card

One by one, the historic buildings on the MUM campus succumbed to Maharishi's architectural theories. When most of them were gone, the bulldozers moved across Wallace Drive and went to work on the old dormitories from the Parsons boom of the sixties.

A "Demolition" page appeared on the MUM Web site, showing thumbnail pictures of forty-eight buildings scheduled for termination. As each one came down, a "no" symbol appeared over the picture.

Eventually, there wasn't much left of the old quad aside from Barhydt Chapel. When MUM announced the chapel's impending demolition, it stirred up bad feelings in town. Barhydt was a local landmark with nostalgic memories for the many Parsons grads in the area.

In an attempt to save the building, the Fairfield city council passed a historic preservation law targeted specifically at the chapel. (Which, after all, was on the National Register of Historic Places thanks to the efforts of MUM itself.) The law held off the wrecking ball, but it couldn't prevent the building's owners from doing what they wanted with their property.

The university offered to sell the chapel to anyone who wanted it for a million dollars. There were no takers.

Barhydt chapel, built in 1911, met its fate in the autumn of 2001.

The university's Demolition and Construction plan promised to replace the "unhealthy" old buildings with new ones that would "promote well-being, good health, and good fortune." During my stay in Fairfield, there weren't many Vedic buildings on campus, but I saw quite a few of them around town. Earl Kaplan's home and business were the most impressive, but there were plenty of smaller houses and offices.

After Books Are Fun, the biggest Vedic office building belonged to Telegroup, a Fairfield legend.

Telegroup began in 1989 when Fred Gratzon, one of Maharishi's entrepreneurial followers, entered the burgeoning telecommunications market. The company started out as a reseller of long-distance service and rapidly expanded into a telecom powerhouse, one of the major success stories of the nineties.

With business booming, Fred and his partner, Cliff Rees, rented office space around Fairfield to accommodate their mushrooming staff. Of course, most of the commercial rental space in town did not comply with the rules of Vedic architecture. Telegroup occupied buildings with doors facing the directions of poverty and mental instability and all negative influences. Nevertheless, business kept booming.

At its peak, Telegroup was a $300 million company that employed over a thousand people around the world. The Fairfield office was the largest employer in the area, with a staff of six hundred people, roughly half of them TM practitioners.

Fred and Cliff, flush with success, built a new corporate headquarters on Highway 1 just north of Fairfield. The sprawling campus, which adheres to all the principles of Maharishi Sthapatya Veda, faces true east.

Shortly after moving into their new building, the dot-com bubble of the nineties burst and Telegroup filed for Chapter 11.

Bobby Roth phoned to ask how my talk with John Hagelin had gone.

"He certainly is a brilliant fellow," I said.

"There's another scientist you should talk to," Bobby told me. "Fred

Travis. He's done some of the most important research on the brain and consciousness and meditation."

Dr. Travis is the chief brain researcher at MUM and quite possibly the most respected scientist in the Movement. Unlike Tony Nader's research on the Vedic hymns and the human nervous system, Travis's work seems almost mainstream.

Ironically, his conservative approach may bring him closer than anyone to a science of enlightenment.

How's your EEG today?" asked Dr. Fred Travis. I placed my fingertips on my brow, rubbed a bit, and said, "Fine, thanks." We both chuckled.

We stood in his laboratory on the MUM campus, a large room filled with computers and electronic paraphernalia. Dr. Travis is tall, skinny, balding—your typical roo, except that, on the day we met, he was wearing a white lab coat instead of a cream suit.

"We've developed a brain model of what's happening in TM," he told me. "Basically, the frontal areas shut down, the thalamus and mid-brain—the nerve center of the brain, the outlet for everything that's rising up into conscious awareness. The mantra sets up a resonant frequency with a part of the thalamus that resonates with the auditory and visual cortex. That adds a dominant input of information. Irrelevant thoughts are not able to interrupt that.

"As soon as you start the mantra, you see this resonant, alpha-wave activity over the whole brain, front, center, and back. The back of the brain is your screen of the mind, where all the raw images come up and you build a concrete image of the world. The center of the brain is your motor strip. The front of the brain is the CEO; it's integrating, planning, sequencing. When we see this alpha-wave activity, very integrated, very coherent, over the whole brain, it means all of those cognitive processes are diminishing. When we transcend, the sensory information diminishes, motor information diminishes. The front of the brain, which is usually questioning and analyzing—all of that diminishes as the mind transcends."

Dr. Travis spoke softly and deliberately. He is obviously on intimate terms with the human brain.

"So, basically," I said, "what you've discovered is a brain model for transcendental consciousness."

"Yes. Then we started looking at what happens outside of meditation. We studied people who just started meditating and people who had been meditating for eight years. What I found is that during TM practice there isn't any difference. At first I thought it didn't make sense, after all 'practice makes perfect,' but TM is different because it doesn't involve effort, you just begin the mantra and the natural tendency of the mind takes the mind to transcendence. There is a difference, though, and that occurs outside of meditation. People who have been meditating longer have more of the EEG pattern of TM practice during activity outside of meditation. So TM is a technique that's quick to master, and when you do it over and over, it's culturing the brain, reintegrating and reconnecting different circuits."

"It's like dipping the cloth," I said, recalling the analogy that Maharishi used to make. The mind is like a piece of white cloth and transcendental consciousness, pure Being, is like a vat of yellow dye. "You dip the cloth and take it out and you do it over and over and the color becomes more pronounced."

"Exactly. When the cloth goes in, it comes out completely yellow each time you hit the transcendent.

"We looked at this in other ways. We studied people who reported witnessing sleep."

Maharishi always said that "witnessing" is a major sign of enlightenment. A person is a witness if he or she identifies with inner Being, pure consciousness, and not with ego or desires or the play of the senses.

"We studied people who have been witnessing sleep—experiencing inner wakefulness throughout the night—for at least a year. We compared them to people practicing TM and non-meditators. We found that people witnessing—living enlightenment so that the transcendent is there all the time—look the same as regular meditators. The difference is in activity.

"What we find in the witnessing group is that the frontal part of the brain is more integrated during activity. This is the part that's connected to every other part of the brain—the sensory area, the emotional area, the motor area—they all send information to the front and the front integrates it and sends it back out. This part becomes more integrated as we move toward enlightenment.

"We also studied how the brain responds to a task. What we found is that the witnessing people waited until they had all the information, and then they responded. The non-meditators prepared to respond too soon, they made mistakes and it slowed them down. They're responding more to what's in the environment than what's inside."

It sounded like what I was hoping for back when I was an MIU student. A scientific way of quantifying spiritual progress. A number that I can look at and see how far I've come.

"So, we've taken all this data and come up with a brain integration scale. On the lower end, the frontal areas of the brain are not integrated and there's less appropriate response to a task. On the upper end, we have greater integration of frontal functioning and more appropriate response.

"For two years now, I've had people come in from the community, take their EEG, see where they fall on the scale, and then talk with them about their experiences. The scale is a very good map of their inner experiences of growth of higher states of consciousness.

"So we're taking all this and coming up with a brain integration report card."

A *report card*? I flashed back to junior high school and gulped hard. Maybe this was more than I wanted.

"It's all based on the idea that experience changes the brain. Every experience . . . they're finding that about 70 percent of brain connections change every day. When you put your attention on something, it changes the chemical composition of the circuits. The information goes through the input fibers, the dendrites expand, the output fibers branch out. The connections between the neurons become more flexible.

"The brain is like a river—it changes every time experience flows through it. So I'm trying to find out how different experiences move you on the brain integration scale.

"I'm taking it to the world. I was in Norway and I recorded data from Olympic gold medalists to see how the peak experiences they have during training affect the brain. I have an opportunity to go to a seminary outside Washington, D.C., and I'd like to look at their brain integration scores and compare them to the level of faith.

"We might look at managers and see how successful managers fall on the brain integration scale. Specifically, managers who act ethically versus managers who just go by the bottom line.

"One of the elements on the brain report card is a moral reasoning scale. It correlated highly with the brain integration scale in the witnessing group. We also look at emotional stability, behavioral coping, categorical thinking—thinking in stereotypes of black and white.

"What it will do is make the idea of inner spirituality into an important scientific variable. A variable that affects performance."

In spite of my phobia about report cards, I liked the idea of getting an evaluation of my state of consciousness. I asked him if he was in need of research subjects. He seemed happy to have a volunteer.

"Please take a seat here at the computer," he said as we walked to a desk with a PC and a small flat-panel display. He held a chair for me and I sat facing the screen.

"We use this cap to attach the electrodes," he said as he fitted the snug cloth covering over my skull. I saw my reflection in the window glass— the red thing on my head looked like a swimming cap, except for the holes positioned over the key parts of my brain.

"The cap makes it easy to get the electrodes into place. We use a little adhesive for each one." He picked up a thick bundle of wires and inserted the first electrode into my cap with a cold squirt of glue. When he was done, the wires trailing from my head made me look like an experiment in a sci-fi movie.

"Just sit easy for a moment," Dr. Travis said as he sat at a computer behind me and revved up the EEG software. His voice was calm and kind. If he's a mad scientist, he's the nicest mad scientist you could wish to meet.

"Now we're going to begin the first task," he said. My job was to watch the screen, listen for a sound, wait until an image appeared, and then click a button on the computer keyboard. After each trial, a message on the screen told me it was okay to blink.

I tried to let go and enter the flow of listening, waiting, and pressing, but every time I jumped the gun and clicked too soon or blinked out of turn I got more and more anxious. The EEG computer was recording my faulty brain waves and comparing them to everybody else in Dr. Travis's database. Olympic athletes. Certified enlightened saints. Grunts who don't even meditate, probably recruited from the alleys of Fairfield after a life of drunken debauchery.

The second task was harder. The computer screen flashed two numbers in quick succession and I had to make a snap choice of the larger number and press the correct button on the keyboard. After a couple dozen trials, I could feel the adrenaline-fueled anxiety radiating from my brain, through my scalp, into the electrodes, and down the bundle of wires into Dr. Travis's database to be added to my permanent record of failure.

"That's great," said Dr. Travis in his gentle, reassuring way. "Now you'll meditate for ten minutes. Jai Guru Dev."

This was the worst of all. I had to meditate, knowing that the machine was watching every thought in my skull. I started thinking the mantra, like I always did, and I tried to hold on to it, but I knew that sooner or later . . .

Damn! It had to be Julie Newmar. I imagined her in full Catwoman regalia, purring and beckoning me into her lair. That'll make a big spike in my EEG. Thoughts of Catwoman tormented me for ten full minutes until Dr. Travis whispered "Jai Guru Dev" and I abandoned my vain attempts at transcendental consciousness.

He showed me a printout of my EEG during meditation.

"This is where you introduce the mantra," he said, pointing to a place where the colored squiggles on the EEG relaxed and flattened in sync. He pointed to a jittery section and told me that it was a thought. He was very nice about it, but I knew that, somewhere deep in his computer database, there was a picture of Julie Newmar with my name on it.

After a couple of months in Fairfield, my collection of books, pamphlets, journals, and videos on TM science and the Maharishi Effect had grown by several inches. One rainy afternoon, I spread it all out on the living room floor and divided it into two piles—the stuff I believed and the stuff I didn't.

I discovered something interesting. Although my level of expertise had come a long way since the seventies, my basic standards hadn't changed much. The belief pile had brain research by Fred Travis and Keith Wallace along with studies on mental and physical health. The skeptical pile had the Maharishi Effect and levitation and southern entrances.

That's how it always was. I could accept that meditation had good effects on the individual. I thought that science could prove it and I wanted that proof for myself.

But I couldn't go for the paranormal stuff. I always thought that there must be simpler explanations—coincidence, gullibility. Besides, it was all kind of cheesy and not very spiritual.

It was comforting to know that I was still basically the same person I'd always been.

Still, I really wanted an independent perspective. There must be somebody outside the Movement who would understand this stuff—a sympathetic physicist or philosopher who'd be willing to examine the Constitution of the Universe and pronounce it bogus or brilliant, science or magic, and tell me why.

I sent e-mail queries to college physics departments, online science forums, and miscellaneous public authorities. One guy in India wrote back to explain that I must be mistaken—scientists who believe in human levitation don't exist. I got several pithy one-liners like this:

"Typical New Age bullshit."

I left three messages on Beth's answering machine and I was pondering a fourth and feeling the same queasiness in my stomach that I got from leaving notes under her door in Good Old 109. Would a fourth note make me look desperate?

I came in from my afternoon run (I was up to five miles a day, farther than I used to go in my student days) and heard the beep I'd been waiting for. I listened to her message, put the phone down, and, before calling her back, I stared at the wall and tried to remember what she looked like the last time I saw her.

It was at MIU in my senior year and Beth had just returned from one of the advanced courses in Europe. I visited her room on the evening she got back. She was all bright grins and fresh silk scarves.

"It was *wonderful*," she said. "The atmosphere was *totally* silent.

"The new techniques are amazing! People are starting to fly! Pretty soon, air traffic controllers will have to learn to direct people instead of airplanes."

She was like a kid with a new toy.

"So . . . what did you do on the course?" I asked.

Suddenly Beth became prim and proper, almost schoolmarmish.

"Well, there was a lot of knowledge," she said in an uptight tone I'd never heard from her before.

"I missed you a lot," I said.

"I missed you, too," she said in her old voice. I pulled her to me and we hugged like old friends. We kissed, briefly at first, then more. I flicked her upper lip with the tip of my tongue. She drew back, frowned, and lowered her eyes.

"I'm sorry," she said, meekly and genuinely. "I really can't do that. I have a higher calling now."

Beth and I were, perhaps, the first couple in history to break up over enlightenment.

Hello! It is *so* great to hear you!" Her voice was just as I remembered it—soft, mellow, faintly southern. A bit tired now, maybe. I asked about her life back home in Kentucky.

"Well . . . it's been a really hard time. I moved back here because of my health. I'm basically living as a hermit these days." Her voice trailed off a bit, but she rallied quickly when the conversation turned to Fairfield.

"That was *such* a wonderful time. I remember staying up late with you and Doug and Jamie and laughing *so* hard."

"I remember the day I met you," I said. "That first day of class when we were supposed to stand up and introduce ourselves and tell how long we'd been meditating. People said 'two years,' 'three years.' One guy had ten years. Then you got up and said 'two months.'"

"I came as soon as I heard about it," she said. "It's like I was waiting my whole life for Maharishi to start a university. I jumped into the Movement with both feet."

She filled me in on the years since our last meeting.

"I went on a lot of courses. Teacher training. Governor training—the sidhis. I taught TM for a while in Kentucky and I initiated a bunch of people. Those were pretty lean times . . . I remember living on dried beans for a couple of weeks. But I figure that I've probably been a monk for quite a few lifetimes, and I was doing something that I really believed in, so it felt right.

"It was really hard work. We were supposed to do things that seemed wonderful but impossible, like finding a mansion in every city where we taught TM."

I'd heard that the Movement was acquiring real estate during the years that Beth was in the field.

"I did get in to see a couple of bankers. I put on my business suit and makeup and I rode downtown on my bicycle with all the trucks and busses whizzing around me. They took me to a huge conference room and I met two guys who looked like villains in a James Bond movie. They were actually really nice, but . . ." she fell into silence.

I asked her if she'd been on the Taste of Utopia course.

"No, but there was the Vedic Science course in New Delhi. They said that you shouldn't go if you had a 'delicate constitution,' but I went anyway. Basically it was in a five-level parking garage with foam and 3,500 people from all over the world and a lot of germs."

I'd never heard anyone talk about this course without noting the high percentage of attendees who got sick. I knew that Beth had lived with health problems for much of her life, and when she mentioned the Delhi course I suddenly felt a stab of concern.

"I was sick almost the entire time," Beth said. "Most of what I remember is waiting in line to see a doctor. I didn't think I was going to make it home."

I inquired about her health.

"Chronic fatigue. Mine seems to be a new variety. I can't go out into the sun, can't tolerate the heat. Medical doctors think it's in my head. I'm seeing a *wonderful* healer, but it costs an arm and a leg.

"I can see the reasons for it in terms of my own psychology. Being allergic to 95 percent of all foods tells you that you're not accepting the world all that well. I'm depending on spirit for everything because I literally do not have the energy to do anything at this point."

She trailed off and then brightened a bit and asked how I was doing. I told her about my life in the software business and my hopes for a new career as a writer.

"I'd love to be a freelance writer," she said. "I had an idea for a beautiful children's story. There's a little girl who gets lost and can't get home until she meets a dragon who teaches her that she can create her own reality. It was so hard to get the feeling of the little girl in the wilderness. I did a candle meditation to go down into her heart. It took hours to get that deep, but it finally came. I knew exactly how she felt!"

"Did you write up any of it?" I asked.

"Oh, no," she said. "I want to do the creative part—the ideas and the feelings. Then I'd give them to the person who does the actual words."

I asked her if she was still active in the Movement.

"I think of my meditating as being part of the Movement. But it was time for me to move on. I'm glad that the Movement was there when it was. It had a big effect on world consciousness. We probably would have blown ourselves up by now if it hadn't been there.

"I think about all the things that we were supposed to do in the Movement. The mansions and everything. It's like it doesn't really matter whether those things worked or didn't work. Whether they happened on the physical level or not, they were being created on another level. The astral level maybe.

"I may not like some things about the Movement. I wish I had all the money in the world so that I could go on all the courses and have all the Ayurveda things. But I'm sure that Maharishi has very good reasons for everything he does, and I trust that."

Her voice trailed off again and I got the feeling that she was getting tired.

"So, did you ever get married?" she asked. I told her about Sarah and our home in the country. She sighed wistfully.

"How about you?" I asked. "Any romantic interests?"

"Heh," she laughed. "I'm a hermit. I don't have much to do with the material world anymore."

I could tell that the conversation was winding down.

"Remember that first time we walked over the bridge by the frat houses?" she asked. "You said, 'Let's go look for dragons,' and of course I couldn't resist that."

I chuckled. "The dragons probably left when they tore down all the buildings."

"Oh, they're still around," she said.

We were quiet for a while.

"Geoff?"

"Yes?"

"I wish you magic," she said.

Chapter 13

Immortality

Day 65.

By the time I arrived at the Raj it was five p.m. and the place was empty. No cars out front. Nobody in the lobby. The whole place was dead quiet.

"Hello?"

Nobody at the front desk; just a small, silver bell that tinkled sadly when I shook it. Everybody must be in the dome levitating.

When I put the bell down I noticed a sheet of paper with my name on it and, next to it, a gold key.

"Welcome to the Raj," it said. "Your room number is 210. Please see the enclosed map for directions to your room. We look forward to meeting you over dinner at seven p.m. in our dining room."

Well, I can't say that I've ever had a luxury hotel to myself before.

When I entered my room the first thing I noticed was the flute music. Slow, mournful notes came from a white cabinet next to the bed. I opened it and found a TV and a black box for the flute. The box had switches with labels that said "Sama Veda" and "Maharishi Open University."

I turned on the TV. The MOU channel was playing a computer-generated cartoon of Maharishi and Guru Dev. The latter sat on his throne with a large orange parasol above him as Maharishi stood to one side with his palms pressed together in respect. A sitar droned in the background as a singer chanted the name of Maharishi's master:

"Bra-ma-nan-da Sa-ra-swa-teeee . . ."

A stream of pink rose petals fell gently from the sky and coalesced into a garland, which Maharishi caught deftly. He bowed toward Guru Dev and the garland fell from his hands and landed before the throne. Then another bunch of rose petals fell from the sky and formed another garland.

The animation looped over and over as the pile of garlands before Guru Dev grew higher and higher.

"Bra-ma-nan-da Sa-ra-swa-teeee . . ."

I switched off the TV and pulled open the curtains to look outside. A reflecting pond beneath my window glowed in the late afternoon sun. Two large white figures—fellow guests in bathrobes?—lazed on the grass beside the water. I squinted at them curiously until one got up and stretched its curved neck and long beak. Big fat white swans. They waddled down to the water and glided across into the reflection of the sun.

The *Cologne Digital Sanskrit Lexicon* gives several meanings for *raj*, including "to illuminate or make radiant." Also: "to reign, be king or chief, rule over, direct, govern."

Most English speakers familiar with the term probably think of this definition from *Microsoft Encarta*: "The British rule of the Indian subcontinent, now the countries of India, Pakistan, and Bangladesh, from 1757 to 1947."

The name of this hotel and its associations always seemed weird to me. Maharishi himself, born in India during the reign of King George V, was a subject of the British Empire for the first three decades of his life. Why would he want this hotel to remind everyone of colonial rule? It's as if Martin Luther King Jr. opened a hotel and called it the Plantation. Eyebrows would go up.

It's not just the name. The architect and interior decorator must have been reading Kipling when they designed the place. On my way to the dining room, I passed the lobby with its chandeliers and opulent floral displays. It was empty, but imagination easily populated it with gentleman officers of the British East India Company in dress whites sipping gin and tonic from a silver tray offered by a native boy in a turban.

As I approached the dining room, I heard clinking glasses and human voices. An efficient young woman in a white apron saw me coming and glanced at her clipboard.

"Geoff?" she asked. I nodded.

"You can join the other guests at the Rejuvenation Table." She pointed through some ferns at a long table where two women sat in the otherwise empty dining hall. "We ask all our Rejuvenation guests to sit together, unless you're taking silence. You can sit by yourself if you're in silence."

"I'm not," I said.

"Have a seat then, and we'll bring your meal right over."

I walked over to the table and introduced myself to my fellow Rejuvenation guests.

"Hi, I'm Veronica," said a trim, bubbly, fair-haired woman of forty-five or so. "This is Josie."

Josie, a dark, statuesque woman who seemed more reserved than her gregarious dining companion, nodded.

"Have a decoction," Veronica said, passing me a small tray of shot glasses filled with brown liquid. "You're supposed to have one before meals."

I tossed it back and got a jolt of pepper and ginger.

"They're good for digestion," Veronica said. "Would you care for some hot water?" she asked as she picked up an alabaster pitcher and filled the delicate teacup by my plate. I examined the steam rising from the cup with distrust. Hot water with no coffee. I took a sip. It was horrible.

"You're supposed to drink it all day," said Josie. "It opens the *shrotis.*"

The shrotis, or channels, make up the body's plumbing system as it was understood by the ancient Indian doctors. According to Ayurvedic theory, you get sick when your shrotis aren't functioning properly. Bad food and an impure lifestyle clog the shrotis with toxins that cause everything from bad breath to cancer. If you're in poor health, the only solution is to flush out the shrotis using traditional methods involving, among other things, lots of hot water.

The woman who had greeted me appeared bearing a large bowl of green liquid, which she placed in front of Josie.

"It's your liquid day?" Veronica asked. Josie nodded and grinned gamely.

"You get a liquid diet every other day," Veronica said to me. "It's not bad. They basically take everything from the meal and put it in a blender." The staff lady returned with my dinner—a plate of grains, vegetables, and blobs of chutney and protein that, added together and divided by the total, would probably produce the green stuff in front of Josie.

"So how long have you been here?" I asked, taking a bite of very mildly spiced tofu.

"Five days," said Veronica. "I was originally planning to drive through California. I had the trip all planned out—I was going to meditate in the redwoods and then drive to Big Sur to see this man who reads earth currents. But my ex-husband suggested I come here. He was here for three weeks and he said it was really good for his stress level. So I followed my higher calling and came to Iowa."

Back in my room, I sat on the bed, sipped hot water from the pitcher on the night table, and reviewed a list of "Orientation Points for Guests."

"The treatments at the Raj are luxurious and, at the same time, powerfully effective. Treatments are generally found to be quite enjoyable. Occasionally, some roughness may occur due to the release of toxins.

"We recommend wearing garment liners at all times during your stay at the Raj. This will protect your clothes from any untimely elimination from the enema therapies.

"Ayurveda recommends an early bedtime—before ten p.m. On the radio in the room there is an option marked 'Sama Veda.' Research has shown that listening to five to ten minutes of these Vedic sounds before going to bed has a very beneficial effect."

I switched on the TV.

"Ay-yaa . . . Ay-yaa. . . ."

I switched off the TV and obeyed the Ayurvedic bedtime recommendation.

Are you comfortable? Do you have enough hot water?"

I smiled and nodded at Hilda, the bubbly, fiftyish representative of Guest Services assigned to orient me.

"Good. If you need more there's a big urn in the alcove down the hall from your room. Is this Thursday?"

"Uh-huh."

She rummaged through a stack of papers in her lap. "You report to the Men's Treatment Facility for your first rejuvenation session this morning. They use a lot of oil, so we recommend you wear clothes that you don't mind getting oily. They'll probably suggest that you leave the oil in your hair after the treatment. If you do, be sure to wear a hat if you go outside. It's really important that you don't get a chill. We have hats for sale in the Herb Room, although they're mostly ladies' summer hats. Is this Thursday?"

"Yes."

She rummaged through the papers again. "You'll be getting the small enema today. You get a liquid diet on the day you have the big enema. That's tomorrow for you. You're staying here for three days?"

"Yes."

"Ohhh . . . you should stay for five. That way you get two of the big enemas."

She picked up the large cloth bag that she'd brought into the conference room and fumbled through it until she found a white plastic doodad with an electrical plug.

"This is your aroma dispenser," she said, handing it to me. "Plug it into one of the wall sockets in your room. It's filled with Vata essence, but we can provide Pitta or Kapha if you prefer. The housekeeping staff fills it up every day when they clean your room."

As she poked through her bag, I asked her how many guests were currently in residence.

"Let's see," she said. "Is this Thursday?"

"Yes."

"Ah. Right now it's just you and Josie and Veronica."

Congratulations, Geoff," said Dr. Lonsdorf after she finished taking my pulse. "You've come a long way. You've lost eighteen pounds and your blood pressure is down. You've corrected the Pitta imbalance you had the last time you were in. We're proud of you."

I smiled back at her. For a brief moment, all my doubts about Ayurveda faded into insignificance. Who cares if there are such things as Pitta and Vata and Kapha? Whether they exist or not, I brought them into balance and made Dr. Lonsdorf proud. What's more, I felt good.

She marked a form and handed it to me. It was titled "Passport to Health and Wholeness Evaluation Report." The form rated my "Nature" ("Pitta Balanced"), "Digestive Strength" ("Irregular"), and two variables called "*Ama* level" and "*Ojas* level." According to the Passport:

"Ama level rates the degree to which impurities have accumulated in your tissues, as indicated by your pulse evaluation. . . . When present, ama blocks the micro-circulatory channels that deliver nutrients to your tissues and carry toxins out of the tissues and out of the body. . . . When ama is eliminated, the body feels lighter, more flexible, aches and pains disappear, and symptoms abate."

As I understand it, ama is a gooey, whitish substance produced by poor digestion. It oozes into your arteries and capillaries and joints and clogs them with poison and makes you sick with arthritis or head colds or cancer.

According to the Passport to Perfect Health and Wholeness, on a scale of zero to four, my ama level is a one. I'm almost totally free of impurities! I basked in Nancy Lonsdorf's smile and silently vowed to attain zero ama.

I have a bit further to go with my ojas, however.

"Ojas level rates the overall level of integration, strength, immunity, and liveliness of your body's inner intelligence as evidenced by your pulse examination."

Another Raj document describes ojas as "the cosmic glue that connects consciousness to matter and supports life itself."

My ojas score on a scale of zero to four is two. In other words, my body's inner intelligence might rate a C+.

"Do you take Amrit?" Dr. Lonsdorf asked me. I shook my head and she told me it was time to start.

Maharishi Amrit Kalash is the "herbal super antioxidant 1,000 times more powerful than vitamin C or E" and the crown jewel of Maharishi's pharmacopoeia. According to the Web site of Maharishi Ayurveda Products:

"Consumers report that Amrit does much more than help keep them healthy. It raises their lives to a new level of happiness, energy, alertness, and inner calm. The same powerful synergy of herbs and fruit that has offered life-enhancing effects for over 5,000 years is confirmed by medical science as today's ultimate antioxidant formula. This formula is still available under the original name, Amrit Kalash, the 'golden cup of immortality,' a name that more and more doctors recommend."

There are two parts to the product—the Ambrosia and the Nectar. A jar of each currently costs $54.98. Of course, there's always a price to pay for immortality.

Before heading to the Treatment Facility, I went back to my room and prepared to get very oily. I took off my Dockers and sweater and put on an old pair of running pants and a T-shirt. When I looked in the mirror I saw my old comfortably grubby self, all ready for rejuvenation.

The Men's Treatment Facility occupied a third of the main floor at the Raj. As I walked in I encountered a sinewy, bearded man in a green smock.

"Geoff? I'm Martin. I'm your Rejuvenation Technician. Please follow me."

He led me down the hall to a door marked RESTING ROOM that opened into a smaller version of my room in the guest wing.

"Please undress and put on this loincloth," he said, pointing to a chair with a scrap of linen draped over it. "There are booties for your feet and you can wrap yourself in this sheet. I'll start the oil and be back in a minute."

Martin seemed very composed and professional, as if he'd been rejuvenating people his whole life.

I donned the wispy loincloth and paper booties and draped the sheet over my shoulders. In the mirror, I looked a bit like Maharishi, a wandering monk in the land of health and wholeness.

Martin returned and led me to the treatment room, a large, bright place with a sunny view of the fields and trees out front. Sesame odor rose from a pan of oil on a hot plate. The treatment room smelled like a Chinese restaurant.

"This is Brett," said Martin, nodding at the third man in the room, "the other technician for your treatment." Like Martin, he was wiry and he wore a green smock. He seemed very somber and never spoke.

"Your first treatment today is called *abhyanga,* a warming treatment with herbalized oil. It lasts about an hour. We'll start with you sitting in this chair while we apply the oil to the upper part of your body, and then move to the table. Brett and I will work in silence. For the maximum benefit, we suggest you keep your eyes closed and place your attention on the strokes."

I sat down and gathered my sheet around me as Brett and Martin knelt on the floor facing me.

"We'll begin by wiping your feet," said Martin. He grasped my right ankle and Brett took my left and they simultaneously lifted my feet, removed the paper booties, and wiped my soles with cotton swabs soaked in alcohol.

Then both men stood and took positions behind me. I closed my eyes as the warm, viscous liquid spilled over my hair and down my neck onto my shoulders like a delicious lava flow. Strong sesame odor filled the room. Then a pair of hands grasped my slick head and worked in the oil with long firm strokes. Martin—I guess it was him—rubbed the muscles of my face and neck up and down over and over as the oil flowed. He stroked my cheeks in clockwise circles, then paused for a second with his fingers poised on my cheekbones, then resumed stroking counterclockwise. He stroked my brow and the muscles under my chin. Then my eye sockets. Then I felt two fingers on my eyelids. They pressed down slightly, made circular strokes, paused, stroked in the opposite direction, paused, and nimbly rose like two grasshoppers leaping at once.

"Now we'll move over to the table," said Martin. "You can leave your sheet on the chair."

How long had it lasted? Ten minutes? I was already loose and flowing and they hadn't made it past my shoulders.

Martin took my arm and helped me up onto a large, solid wooden table.

"We'll begin with you on your back."

Martin and Brett stood on each side of the table with ladles of the warm oil, which they drizzled on my legs from my feet to my waist. I closed my eyes again as four hands slid up and down my legs, pausing at the tips of my toes and stroking again in tight harmony. They never spoke or communicated in any way that I could tell, yet every stroke was perfectly synchronized as if Brett and Martin were a single, four-handed being. They must have practiced for ages to get the technique down.

The oil kept flowing. How much? Gallons? They rubbed it in and my skin kept soaking it up. The smell of sesame filled the whole universe as they poured and poured and massaged my legs and chest and arms. Eventually it was time to roll over. As they stroked my back from shoulders to toes I felt like I was dissolving into the oil.

This must be what life was like for the maharajas in old India—plenty of cheap labor to massage you head to toe hour after hour. I briefly wished that Brett and Martin were women, possibly starlets from the Indian cinema with dark eyes and rubies in each nostril. Something would be missing, though. The whole situation was so extremely non-masculine that it opened the door for a new and unexpected masculine feeling to emerge—a comradeship of the body, a shared experience of life at the basic level of skin and muscle and simple movement. Just three guys tending to the male body in a matter-of-fact way.

A bird sang outside the window. Such a pure and beautiful sound.

The hands paused one last time on the soles of my feet and then departed. Brett left the room quietly.

"Please roll over on your back for the next treatment," said Martin. "It's called *shirodhara*," he said as he attached a metal pan to a rod suspended above my head. "I'll be running a stream of cool oil over your forehead. It's very relaxing. The treatment lasts about twenty minutes."

He filled the pan with oil and placed a folded towel over my eyes. Then I heard a metallic clink as the reservoir opened and the oil touched my forehead and trickled down my scalp and flowed off the back of my head. The stream went on and on without interruption. I occasionally heard clinking noises behind me as Martin refilled the pan above my head.

I'd seen photographs of shirodhara in promotional literature for the Raj and thought it was the dumbest thing I'd ever seen. Once the stream of oil started, however, I wanted it to go on forever. The gentle rain obliterated my sense of time, dissolved what was left of my body, and filled me with contentment and pleasure.

Your last treatment is called *basti*," Martin said. "It's an enema of herbalized oil."

We were back in the Resting Room. I was lying on the bed with a hot water bottle under the small of my back as Martin placed another hot water bottle on my stomach. "It's said to make the body more receptive," he explained.

He left the room to "make up the basti" and I rested while flute music played in the background. It was the same mournful, repetitive music that was playing in my room when I arrived. I wondered if the music ever changed.

Martin returned with the enema bag, removed the hot water bottles, and told me to roll over on my side.

"Now, this basti is small, but it's sneaky," he said. "You may think you've expelled it all when there's still some left. You can carry some of it around in you without any problem, but it may come out unexpectedly. That's why we provide lots of garment liners. You'll find a stack of them in the bathroom. I'll insert the tube now."

As the tube went in, I wondered what it's like to be a professional enema technician. Endless anuses day after day.

When he was done administering the enema, Martin instructed me to lie on my back as he placed a bolster under my legs. "It's said that this position provides the most efficient rejuvenation," he explained.

Who, exactly, said that? The ancient Ayurvedic texts? Maharishi? I imagined the nurse at my HMO giving me a shot of penicillin and telling me "It's said to be beneficial against microorganisms."

Martin unfolded a blanket over me and tucked me in before taking his leave. On his way out, he paused and looked in my direction with his eyes cast down. "This job gives me great satisfaction," he said softly. "I am especially glad to offer treatment to those who can appreciate it."

That evening I floated into the dining hall and beamed at Veronica and Josie as I threw back my decoction and savored the tickle of ginger in my throat.

"You left the oil on your hair," observed Veronica. "Josie does, too."

Indeed, Josie's black hair was slicked back like a greaser's, while Veronica's remained dry and fluffy. I recalled Martin telling me "It is said that leaving the oil in the hair provides the maximum benefit." Perhaps, but it feels odd to put on nice clothes and walk into a good restaurant with the equivalent of three tubes of Dippity-Do on your head.

Dinner arrived and Veronica smiled at her bowl of pea-green liquid. Then she closed her eyes and held her hands over the bowl with her palms about three inches above the rim. Her lips moved silently. She flowed with the energy currents of her liquid diet for about twenty seconds, then broke the circuit, picked up a spoon, and took a sip.

"We learned TM today," she said cheerfully.

I smiled and nodded supportively. "What was it like?" I asked.

"It's very nice," Veronica said, seeming less than her usual enthusiastic self. She might have felt an inner need to be positive after purchasing an expensive mantra.

Josie looked seriously perplexed. "Do you think it's a religion?" she asked quietly. It was more than I'd heard her say before.

"Well . . ." I said, nodding my head from side to side to indicate ambivalence.

"They keep saying it isn't a religion," Josie continued, her voice growing louder and firmer, "but there's the ceremony and the pictures of Maharishi and Guru Dev everywhere." I nodded. That always bugged me. "And the people here seem to treat it like a religion, like it's the center of everything to them."

"Well," I said, "that's always been a controversial issue. It sure does look like a religion at times."

"They told us that there's no solution to anything except TM. I don't believe that. I believe that if you've got a problem, you try to fix it, and if that doesn't work you turn to God and let Him take care of it."

I nodded again. Josie was on a roll.

"Do you think it's a cult?" she asked, looking at me very intently. I tried to appear as bland and noncommittal as possible.

⌒

If this is Friday, it must be time for my big enema. That's how it works at the Raj. You get two kinds of enemas—the small "nutritious" enema and the big "cleansing" enema—on alternate days.

My treatment began with an abbreviated version of the oil massage I'd had the day before. Then, instead of pouring oil on my forehead, Martin and Brett rubbed me all over with big pads soaked in milk.

"That was my favorite treatment," Veronica told me over lunch. I jealously eyed the plate of solid food before her—real grains of rice and cubes of protein instead of the green mush in my pathetic bowl.

"It really is okay," said Veronica as I took my first bite. "They blend it coarsely so it still has some texture. And you can have as much of it as you want."

Actually, the soup was quite good. Two months ago I would have loaded it down with salt and chili powder. Now, after six weeks of the Ayurvedic diet, that didn't even sound good. Subtle flavors and textures seemed much more interesting and satisfying than they used to.

As I rolled the bits of asparagus and potato around my palate, Josie and Veronica and I discussed the day's treatments.

"I had Vedic Vibration today," said Josie. "It's nice. Relaxing. I think it's been good for my health issues."

Josie explained that she'd had a neck injury a few years ago that still gave her a lot of pain. It's the kind of chronic condition that Vedic Vibration is supposed to alleviate. According to the Vedic Vibration Web site an Ayurvedic pundit "whispers within himself or herself some specific sounds traditionally chosen for the indicated health concerns and then administers them by blowing on and/or touching the affected area of the body. Given her alternatives—painkillers and surgery—it's easy to understand that Josie would rather sit in a comfortable chair while a pundit breathes on her. Of course, like everything else in Maharishi's health-care system, relief from chronic pain isn't cheap. Vedic Vibration therapy goes for $900for each disorder.[22]

The topic changed to life after the Raj.

"I hope I can keep the diet going," Josie said. "My kids are never going to eat stuff like this."

"My son went off the program way too fast," said Veronica. Her son and her ex-husband spent three weeks at the Raj, which must have cost upward of ten grand.

"We had dinner together right after he got back. He said to me, 'You know all those things I'm not supposed to eat? Like chicken?' Then he ate a piece of chicken. Then he said, 'You know how I'm not supposed to drink carbonated beverages?' and he drank a Coke. He got *so* sick."

"I heard about this one woman who stayed here," added Josie. "She was on the airplane flying home and she ate a bag of M&Ms. They had to take her from the airport to the hospital."

"It's hard to live a Vedic life in the real world," I added.

Since it was our last evening together, we posed for a group photo in the garden outside the dining room. Johnny—the resident Ayurvedic chef who used to cook for Maharishi—photographed his guests arm in arm, grinning like the Three Musketeers of Rejuvenation, standing among formal trees and shrubs framed by the fence that shields the southern end of the building from evil.

The photo shows Josie voluptuous in black with slicked-back hair and an expression slightly strained by years of chronic pain. Veronica has the face and body of a wispy pilgrim and the clothing of Beverly Hills. I look happier than I have in ages.

On the morning of my departure, I was folding a pair of socks when I heard swans hooting outside my window. I added the socks to the pile in my suitcase and smiled.

So this is Maharishi's version of what life should be like. I can handle it. After three days of rejuvenation treatment and two months of the Ayurvedic diet, I can honestly say that I felt fantastic—clear-headed, light, energetic, and at peace.

The most unexpected reward was the vividness of everything. The fine-grained details of life—little things like the ripples in the reflection of the swan on the mirror-perfect pond—leapt into full clarity. Each moment offered these things, and the moments lingered. Maybe this timeless feeling is what Maharishi means by immortality. I didn't care. I just wanted the world to stay that way.

When I was done packing, Hilda stopped by to say farewell. "I see you're leaving," she said. "I'll have the kitchen staff pack you a box lunch. Let's see . . . is this Saturday?"

Chapter 14

The Enlightenment Course

Fairfield is a crucible of spirituality. Twenty percent of its population moved there to meditate. Most of them have practiced TM and other techniques of inner development for decades. You would expect to find highly evolved souls on every street corner.

When I was in Professor Fred Travis's EEG lab, I asked him about the enlightened subjects he studied in his brain research. He told me that he had recruited a handful of people from the Fairfield TM community who exhibited "witnessing" and other signs of Cosmic Consciousness. I asked him if he could introduce me to any of them.

"They like to maintain their privacy," he said, which I could certainly understand. He did offer to pass on my name and number to his subjects the next time he saw them, but I never heard anything.

I got a better lead from Rick Archer, the moderator of the Fairfield Life discussion group.

"We have this neat meeting every Wednesday night. It's a *satsang*.[15] There are about thirty people who meet in a living room and have a discussion. A good percentage of the people in that room have awakened, whatever you make of that. I don't claim to be one of them, but I get absolutely high as a kite from participating. It's shifted my experience more than anything in the last year. The day after, I just sit and have clear transcending while I meditate.

"Everybody has a Movement background and a good number of people in the room have gone on to other things. Out of respect to those who still feel strong allegiance to the Movement, we don't discuss controversial things. We're just talking about our experiences.

"There have been three or four or five people who have undergone awakenings as a result of those meetings. People are very open and honest."

The address Rick gave me turned out to be a nondescript apartment building not far from the MUM campus. Following his instructions, I walked in the front entrance and looked for the apartment with lots of shoes parked outside.

The door was open, so I removed my shoes and joined the other early arrivals sitting in chairs arranged in a circle around the small living room. We were what you'd expect for a group of roos—middle aged and gray but generally healthy and smiling. There wasn't a cream-colored suit or gold tie in the place.

I took a seat as the rest of the group trickled in by ones and twos. It was a comfortable crowd of people who had known each other for a long time. I checked out each new arrival for signs of Cosmic Consciousness. The tall, lanky guy in jeans? The matronly woman with her hair in a bun? None of them seemed especially holy or charismatic. I wondered if they were looking at me and wondering the same thing.

One guy poked his head in the door and asked, "Is this the meeting where everybody thinks they're enlightened?" He got a happy roomful of laughter.

Somebody handed me a list of guidelines, which were mostly about where to park your car and put your shoes. The stated purpose of the meeting was to "discuss life." That was about it.

There was no group leader or protocol. At eight p.m., a friendly woman in jeans spoke up, apparently continuing a topic from last week.

"I see these experiences, these lives, I guess, all laid out before me. And it's like I can enter into any one of them and be that thing, fully occupy it. But I'm also the one looking down and seeing them all at once."

People nodded and said "yes." There was plenty of discussion, although some of it was difficult for me to follow. I'd obviously entered a conversation that had been going on for a long time.

Rick Archer—a sharp, lively guy with a friendly face—interrupted the conversation at one point.

"Since we have some newcomers," he said, "perhaps somebody would like to tell their story."

The volunteer was a fiftyish guy who looked as ordinary as they come. It's hard to relate his story without including a bunch of personal details. Suffice to say that he was in a room admiring the furnishings when:

"... it came to me: *thou art that.* I had this complete identification with what I was seeing. There was no separation; it was all part of the same wholeness.

"Everything came together in a kind of infinite correlation. But it was all . . ." he paused for a moment as if he were looking for the right words to describe the ineffable, "all totally ordinary. I thought 'Is this really what Maharishi experiences?' It seemed so simple and natural. Then I thought, 'Wait a minute, that's what he's been saying all along.'" There were some chuckles from the crowd.

"I sort of looked away, and then looked back, expecting that it would be over, but it was still there. And it's still there now. It's totally normal, but amazing and wonderful and satisfying."

There were questions and further sharing of experiences. Several people appeared to speak authoritatively from the standpoint of enlightenment, while others shared my lack of understanding.

"I am lost," one woman said.

"Who is this *I*?" somebody asked, to general amusement. Several group members prompted the lost woman to reflect on the experience of being lost and the question of who has the experience. I felt that they were drawing her out, leading her on. Finally, she lapsed into a reflective silence.

During the lull in conversation, I noticed that all the thoughts in my mind had ceased. Everything was perfectly still, within and without. A warm feeling of happiness came to me, a sense of pleasure just sitting in the room with the people around me.

When the meeting ended, I walked out into the chilly Iowa night feeling, as Rick put it, "high as a kite."

When the weather gets warm, chairs appear on the sidewalks outside restaurants and coffee shops, turning Fairfield once again into an unlikely outpost of café society. I sat outside Le Petit Paris, an organic French restaurant, with a mug of coffee and no concerns in the world. The sky was deep and blue.

I thought about the satsang and the fellow who described his experience of waking up into enlightenment. He looked around and everything was perfect. Everything is part of the same whole.

"I saw the tree," he said, "and it wasn't like I was the tree looking back at myself, but I recognized that 'I am that and the tree is that.'"

The trees on the Fairfield town square were rustling in a refreshing breeze.

"People come away from the satsang and they start having incredible experiences," another person at the meeting said. I suppose that's the point. People go there after meditating for thirty years. They think they're headed nowhere, on a permanent plateau, and then they hear some guy talking about trees and . . . bingo!

Well, maybe that's how it'll work for me. Maybe I can *decide* that it'll work that way for me.

It was an exceptionally gorgeous day. I eased back in my chair and took a sip of coffee and enjoyed the clouds. I didn't need anything more than what I had. The moment was just right, and the moment would always be there. I could have it whenever I wanted it because, really, there's nothing else.

Could this be . . . ?

I looked at the trees. Beautiful, satisfying, perfect even. But it wasn't "I am that." The tree and I were still as separate as the scientist and the specimen on either side of the microscope.

My perfect moment might be nothing more than the smug satisfaction of a beautiful day and a sidewalk café. Even so, it was awfully nice.

I thought of the satsang again and the fellow describing his first moments of enlightenment. "Perfect correlation," he said. Maybe that's what'll do it for me.

I looked into the street. A van drove by as a woman stepped off the curb across from the restaurant. The van slowed down to make way for the woman crossing the street. They seemed to be moving effortlessly along set paths, as if they were sliding down clear plastic chutes set into the air. At the point where the two paths curved together and almost touched, the van stopped and the woman waved at the driver.

The paths diverged; I saw the trajectories in the air almost as clearly as the van and woman following them. The woman stepped onto the curb and the van accelerated down the street. It was all perfectly right—all the other events in the world going back forever were lined up in just the right way to bring the woman and the van together to exchange a wave.

I smiled.

"Wait a minute," I thought. "That's predestination. That can't be right."

I closed my eyes and shook my head a bit. Then it was all just cars and people walking around. But it was still very nice.

I took another sip of coffee and admired the clouds. I heard a car approach. Then another. The first car drove into view and the second one came just behind it. Perfect . . . like marbles falling down a chute and lining up in a neat row.

I smiled again. Maybe this would be it?

The cars passed and I enjoyed the clouds for a while. I heard another car approach. I couldn't see it yet, but I knew that it was a banged-up sedan and the driver was a long-haired guy wearing a red ball cap.

The car drove into view. It was just as I'd pictured it, ball-capped driver and all. The fact that I knew in advance was perfect, too.

I finished my coffee. The people and cars seemed to be moving around at random again.

As I got up to leave, I tossed my cup into a waste basket. Looking at the empty cup among the pop cans and fast-food wrappers, I realized that my experience of infinite correlation might just be one way that the caffeine molecule operates on the human brain. What's more, my psychic prediction was well within the boundaries of imagination and probability.

Still, it really was a gorgeous day.

I phoned Sarah to tell her how great I felt.

"I'm afraid you're not coming home," she said.

I remember watching the *Merv Griffin* show in '75 when Maharishi was the guest of honor. Clint Eastwood strode on stage and walked up to Maharishi's couch, pausing to open his suit jacket and reach in as if to pull out Dirty Harry's .44 Magnum. Instead, he produced a flower and handed it to Maharishi. TM initiations soared to 35,000 a month.

Most of the TM stars are long gone, but a handful remain. It is appropriately weird that the most visible TM celebrities are alumni of the *Twin Peaks* TV show.

Richard Beymer, who played Benjamin Horne in *Peaks,* is a genuine Hollywood star. He appeared in *The Diary of Anne Frank, The Longest Day,* and *West Side Story,* in which he played Tony, the male lead opposite Natalie Wood. Beymer's a long-time meditator who was backstage during the *Merv* show. He has home movie footage of the celebrity meditators waiting to pay their respects to the Indian holy man who brought them inner peace.

There's also Heather Graham, Annie Blackburn on *Peaks*, also known for her roles in *Boogie Nights* and *Austin Powers*. Graham was on the cover of the *Time* magazine issue on meditation in August of 2003.

Then there's the maestro himself, David Lynch. The director of *Peaks* and films such as *Blue Velvet* and *The Elephant Man* is a longtime TMer and, currently, a member of the Board of Trustees of Maharishi University of Management.

When I told Bobby Roth that I was a huge *Peaks* fan, he asked me if I'd like to talk to the man himself. I tried not to sound too much like an overheated fanboy when I said yes.

I spoke with Lynch by phone at his office in Los Angeles. At the time, he was a recent graduate of the Enlightenment Course, a one-month advanced training program conducted by Maharishi at his home in the Netherlands. In the Movement community at large, the Enlightenment Course is also known as the "millionaire's course." That's because of the course fee: $1 million.

"I became interested in meditation, say, in '69 or '70," he told me. "It took a while. I was very interested in starting meditation, but I didn't know which one to do. I talked to my sister one day and she said that she started Transcendental Meditation. There was something in the sound of her voice. It was an intuitive thing. I just said, 'That's what I want,' and I've been meditating twice a day ever since."

Lynch speaks with a folksy, boyish enthusiasm that would be unusual and refreshing anywhere. It must be rare indeed for Hollywood.

"How have TM and the sidhis influenced your life and work?"

"Well, you know, in the first two weeks of meditating, anger left me. The enjoyment of life gets so great. Every little thing is fun to do. And the things that were killing you are receding. So, it's money in the bank, I say, to add meditation to your life. Dive into the treasury every day."

I asked him how he went from being a private meditator to being publicly involved with Movement organizations such as MUM.

"I didn't really talk about meditation because there were so many misunderstandings about it floating around out there. If people were close to me I'd talk about it, but I wouldn't talk about it in public.

"Then Maharishi came out with the Maharishi Effect and at first I just couldn't believe that it could be true, but then I knew it could be true. Then I figured it's gonna happen next week, you know, it's just perfect. Then it didn't happen, so I figured that I'd better start talking and doing something because I really believe in it.

"I am not enlightened. I am just a foot soldier. So I get out there and say why I love meditation and what it can do for me and human beings and the world."

I asked about the Enlightenment Course.

"It had a profound influence on me. I consider myself really lucky to have been there and I'm still recovering from it. It was really beautiful. You know, it blew some holes in things. I'm still trying to figure it all out. It's like you're driving along happily enough at 45 miles an hour and the engine is running pretty good and then suddenly it's a giant 12-cylinder engine and you're going along at 400 miles an hour."

"I understand that you're involved with a project to teach TM in the public schools."

"We're forming a David Lynch Foundation for Consciousness-Based Education and World Peace. I hope to raise money for those two things because they go hand in hand. Dr. John Hagelin is setting up a university of peace in Washington, D.C., and in India, Maharishi wants a supergroup there. I feel like the penny's gonna drop one of these days and people are gonna support this.

"The Maharishi Effect is a real thing in my book, and the sooner we get it going the sooner people can start to enjoy life on this planet."

The sun was going down as I sat on my back porch and placed my laptop on a little plastic table next to my mug of Pitta Cooling Tea. Before turning on the computer, I looked at my reflection in the dark screen. I'd lost a lot of weight. If you stuffed me in a cream-colored suit, I'd pass for a Governor of the Age of Enlightenment.

"What am I doing this for?" I thought.

If my goal was to reclaim my youthful lifestyle, I made it. I got more exercise, fewer calories, and better sleep. I spent two hours a day doing yoga, meditation, and breathing exercises. I hung out with spiritual people.

I wasn't enlightened by the Movement's gold standards—I wasn't witnessing sleep or experiencing unity. I was still separate from the rest of creation.

"Why did I get into this stuff in the first place?" I wondered.

Back in the day, when we were all full of *Be Here Now* and *The Autobiography of a Yogi*, enlightenment didn't need any excuses. There it was, offering itself as a better way of life. Who wouldn't go for it?

If somebody back then had bothered to ask why I wanted to be enlightened, I probably would have said something about inner peace or experiencing the divine or maybe reaching my full potential.

Was I really looking for escape? A door leading out of a miserable adolescence in an unfriendly part of the world?

Maybe that's why I got back into the whole thing as an adult. Escape from a dead-end life in corporate purgatory.

"Oh well," I thought. "It's more interesting. And the food is better."

I fired up the computer and searched for information about Sthapatya Veda, the ancient Indian science of sacred architecture. It's interesting what you find when you go past the Movement's party line to sources in academia or Indian religion. The euphemisms ("influences," "negativity") drop off and you get the straight dope. On Wikipedia, I found a list of cardinal directions with the corresponding deities. South is the direction of Yama, Lord of Death.

Wikipedia had the following for *rakshasa*:

Traditionally, a rakshasa . . . is a demon or unrighteous spirit in Hinduism. . . . Many Rakshasa were particularly wicked humans in previous incarnations. Rakshasas are notorious for disturbing sacrifices, desecrating graves, harassing priests, possessing human beings, and so on. Their fingernails are poisonous, and they feed on human flesh and spoiled food. They are shapechangers and magicians, and often appear in the forms of humans, dogs, and large birds.

A few doors down, I heard a woman's voice sobbing. There were a lot of Movement people in my neighborhood, all living in houses that lack the proper defenses against evil. They'd live in Vedic houses if they could afford them, but a lot of Movement people just scrape by.

The sobbing stopped. I heard a chittering noise. Squirrels? Or maybe something huge and ancient with sharp fangs. Some huge thing, groping from house to house, looking for a southern door that some idiot left open as an invitation to disease and death.

I chuckled in the darkness. Would the Lord of Death care about the orientation of the real estate?

I finished off my Pitta tea as the moon rose. It would give me enough light to run a few more miles before ten p.m. and bedtime.

Chapter 15

Excommunication

It would be nice if you could open the yellow pages and find a consulting physicist to answer your questions about quantum mechanics. I tried very hard to find a non-Movement scientist willing to talk about the Maharishi Effect. I came up empty until I contacted the Committee for the Scientific Investigation of Claims of the Paranormal, the group that publishes *Skeptical Inquirer* magazine.

They put me in touch with Dr. Victor Stenger, a physicist at the University of Hawaii and the author of *Physics and Psychics* and *The Unconscious Quantum*. He became interested in paranormal claims about quantum mechanics when the topic became hot in the 1970s thanks to popular books like *The Tao of Physics*.

"I'm kind of all by myself in this field," Dr. Stenger told me. "Most physicists don't think about the mystical claims of quantum mechanics. I'm the only one who really went into them in any depth and tried to show what they're saying rather than dismiss them out of hand."

I told Stenger about my conversation with John Hagelin.

"Hagelin says it's possible for people doing TM to directly influence the unified field of physics," I said. "He says that it's actually a field of consciousness. All the phenomena of nature—gravity, matter, energy—come

out of a unified field of consciousness. We can control those things because our human consciousness is connected to the unified field."

"I remember when Maharishi put out big ads in papers about the unified field in the late seventies," he said. "There are a lot of theories of
Grand Unification. The simplest one, the one that Maharishi was promoting, made a very specific prediction—that the proton would decay.
People set up big experiments all around the world and everybody expected to find proton decay, but they didn't find it. So that Grand Unified
theory, the one in Maharishi's ads, turned out to be false. I found that
very amusing."

"So when Hagelin talks about the unified field as an established fact of
physics . . ."

"No. That's dead wrong. Not only is it not an established fact, the simplest version of it was ruled out about twenty years ago."

"So when he talks about the unified field, it's not only premature to
talk about it as a field of consciousness, it's premature to talk about it existing at all."

"Yeah."

Dr. Stenger doubts that there's any connection at all between quantum
mechanics and consciousness. He says that people who make this association are misreading an interpretation of quantum theory known as
Copenhagen.[16]

"That refers to the connection between the observer and the observed," he explained. "For example, you could measure the position of a
body, a particle. According to Copenhagen, that position really doesn't
exist until you measure it. It's the very act of measurement that gives the
body its position."

"Is that the 'collapse of the wave function' that Hagelin talks about?" I
asked.

"Yeah. The wave function defines the position of a body. Before a particle is observed, the wave function covers the whole universe—the particle could be anywhere. Then you measure it and there's this kind of

collapse—the wave changes its shape all over and the particle collapses to the size of the detector and you know where it is.

"So there's a very close connection between the act of observation and the thing being observed. That's the source of the notion that the mind makes reality."

"When I talked to Hagelin," I said, "he suggested that the collapse of the wave function might explain the Maharishi Effect. The idea is that you've got a group of people meditating in one place who create effects far away. They might lower the number of war deaths in another country."

"That's what Einstein called 'spooky action at a distance' because the wave function technically collapses all over the universe. But the question is what you mean by that. You get into trouble when you assume that the wave function is real. As far as I'm concerned, it's just a theoretical construct. Nobody's ever seen a wave function.

"The example I like to give is winning the lottery. Suppose I'm in Hawaii and I enter the New York lottery. The probability is one in ten million. Suppose they roll the ball in New York and I win. The probability goes instantaneously from one in ten million to unity.

"Now, Hagelin would say that my wave function has instantaneously collapsed. But I have no way of knowing that or spending the money until I get some signal from New York. And the fastest that a signal can travel is the speed of light; it's not instantaneous.

"To say that my wave function has collapsed simultaneously all over the universe . . . well, that's just a way of talking. It has no effect on things, it has no detectable consequence, no way that it can be used in any way. So what is it? Is it an element of reality? I'd say no, it's just our own invention that we use to describe some observations."

Dr. Stenger explained that the Copenhagen interpretation—the source of quantum mysticism—is losing favor among physicists. A newer interpretation known as "decoherence" avoids the problems of Copenhagen.

"The idea is that you don't need an observer interacting with a quantum system. The environment itself can do this. For example, suppose you have a beam of gamma rays going through the air. The gamma rays quickly decohere by scattering off the air molecules. Every time they scatter it's like making a measurement. It's equivalent to being observed. There doesn't have to be a mind involved. There certainly doesn't have to be any kind of human action involved.

"There's really nothing spooky about it all. The general consensus of physicists over the years is that quantum mechanics is a theory and it works. The rest of these issues are just metaphysics that really don't matter. It's like asking how many angels can dance on the head of a pin."

As far as I can tell, the only independent researchers who have seriously analyzed the studies on the Maharishi Effect are two professors at the University of Iowa—sociologist Barry Markovsky and philosopher Evan Fales. In a paper published in the sociology journal *Social Forces,* Fales and Markovsky reported major holes in the Jerusalem study. The study correlates the number of people practicing the TM sidhis with variations in the intensity of the war in Lebanon. However:

"[The Movement researchers] make no mention of the many widely publicized military and political events that may have both influenced the Lebanon war and induced meditators' patterns of participation. Many such events occurred around the midpoint of the study, coinciding with the wildest fluctuations in group size and war intensity."[17]

According to Fales and Markovsky, the Jerusalem study omitted other significant factors. Several important Jewish holidays occurred during the experiment and a significant percentage of the Israeli population left the country on vacation.

Fales and Markovsky offered to do an independent analysis of the raw data in the Jerusalem experiment. This is a typical procedure in academic science, and the Iowa researchers had the credentials for the job. After numerous requests to the lead author of the Jerusalem study, Markovsky wrote:

"I have been trying for nearly half a year to get the data from the MIU researchers, to no avail as yet."

For another opinion outside the Movement, here's Jorge Lopez—one of the physicists who worked with John Hagelin on a unified field theory called Flipped SU(5):

"It's absolutely ludicrous to say that TM has anything to do with Flipped SU(5)."[18]

Hagelin might say that his former colleague suffers from the "entrenched prejudice" of the scientific community, from the "bias" in favor of the "myth of materialism."

As a matter of fact, however, the old-paradigm establishment has shown Maharishi a surprising amount of hospitality. For example, it's interesting to read the article on the Jerusalem experiment in the *Journal of Conflict Resolution*. Defending his decision to publish such an unusual article, the Journal's editor had this to say:

"Even non-Marxists would hardly find it acceptable to dismiss a piece of research simply because it originated in Marxist assumptions. . . . It is vital to uphold normal scientific standards. But the practice of censorship in science, as in more overtly political realms, can be very unedifying . . . Galileo was censored because his views offended the precepts of religious authorities."

There's even been some funding. In 1999, the National Institutes of Health awarded MUM an $8 million grant to "study the effectiveness of Maharishi Consciousness-Based Health Care approaches for the treatment and prevention of cardiovascular disease."[19]

To my knowledge, nobody outside the Movement has attempted to replicate any of the studies on the Maharishi Effect. An independent researcher would have to recruit hundreds or thousands of Yogic Flyers, Maharishi's core followers. That's easy enough for the Movement's in-house scientists, but well-nigh impossible for somebody outside the fold.

The Movement continues to promote the Maharishi Effect, and it has achieved some pop-culture visibility thanks to Hagelin's appearance in the cult film *What the Bleep Do We Know!?* As science, however, it may be running out of steam. Of forty-eight studies on the Maharishi Effect cited on the MUM Web site, most are from the late eighties and only two have dates later than 2000.

I'm going on the Amma tour this summer," Doug said. "She does it every year. She starts in California and winds up in New York, hugging people coast to coast. The energy is incredible. It's like the Movement used to be."

We were walking along the river in Iowa City near the coffeehouse where Doug worked on weekends. Ducks paddled on the leaden water and college students in woolen caps and white earphones scurried around us.

"Isn't it risky to be involved with another group?" I asked, recalling the paranoia of the old days, the stories of people who strayed too far from Movement purity and wound up on the black list.

"Well . . ." he said softly, "they already kicked me out."

"Huh?"

"They found out that I was going to see the lady saints."

The lady saints are female gurus who periodically pass through Fairfield. Amma is the best known, but there are several others.

"They called me up and told me to come into the program office on campus. So I showed up and they asked me about it and I said that I didn't think it was a problem, I didn't think there was any conflict. But they said there was. They cancelled my dome badge. I'm officially excommunicated."

"So . . . you can't meditate in the dome."

"Nope."

"That's . . . wrong," I said.

"Well, yeah. I was pretty shook up by it."

There was a bit of a catch in his voice. The Movement had been his community since he was a teenager.

"But I'm not the only one," he continued. "Lots of people got black-balled over the years for all kinds of stuff. I guess I can see it if you go public in a big way, like people who split off and set up their own organi-zations. But a lot of the time it's just minor stuff like going to the wrong meetings. My feeling is that what you do on your own time should be your own business, but that's not the party line."

"Doug . . . that sucks. You're not a threat. It's not like you've turned against Maharishi or anything."

"Oh *God* no. He pretty much shaped me from the beginning. I'll al-ways be grateful for that."

It was late when I drove back to Fairfield. I stewed over my friend's dis-charge for the whole sixty miles and I arrived in town thoroughly pissed off. The streets were empty and the houses were dark. I passed the front entrance of MUM and turned onto the street that ran along the southern border of the university and led to my apartment. In the dim light, I could barely make out the gray barrier that separated the university from the rest of the town.

I parked on a side street and walked back to the edge of campus, where I found the chain-link fence they'd erected to keep out Yama, Lord of the Dead. I walked up to the fence and looked through it at the remains of the old quad. In my day, you could walk straight from your dorm through the quad and into the town square in a few minutes. The fence added a big detour.

I turned my back to the fence and looked south. It was cold and last autumn's dead leaves blew around my feet. If the rakshasas were going to come for me, they'd never have a better opportunity. I peered into the darkness and opened my imagination to every snap and rustle that came on the wind. If any demons showed up, at least I'd know there was some point to the fence other than vanity and ignorance.

Only the wind.

I walked along the perimeter to the intersection where Highway 1, the town's major north-south artery, divided the campus in half. The fence ended at the sidewalk, of course. The dumbest rakshasa in hell could march right in.

I thought of continuing my walk, but it was getting cold and I'd seen what I came for. The Movement put up a barrier to keep out the god of death and failed. It worked on me, however. I had no desire to go in any farther.

The knocking got louder and louder. It rose up from the depths and pounded in my head as I fought the shadows and clawed at the sweat-soaked sheets. I jerked up in bed with a gasp. The shadows receded into the bright yellow sunshine that filled my bedroom.

I crawled out of the futon on my hands and knees. The noise started again. I computed the direction—south—before realizing that somebody was knocking at the door.

I pulled on a bathrobe and went to the door expecting, in my half-awake state, the forces of hell. It was my landlady.

"Good morning," she said with a smile, "I stopped by to see if you were planning to stay on another month."

"Um, I'm not sure yet. Can I let you know in a couple of days?"

When she left I made some coffee and sat down at my kitchen table and thought about my time in Fairfield. I certainly wasn't done with the spiritual search that brought me to Iowa. The physical part—the diet and exercise—I could do back in Wisconsin or anywhere. I could certainly find a supportive spiritual community in Madison. As for TM, it's definitely nice to meditate in a group, but it means getting in your car and using up a good chunk of the day. The longer I stayed in Fairfield, the more I reverted to my old habit of solitary meditation.

There was still one thing I hadn't done. Practically everyone I met in Fairfield, on or off the program, told me "You should get the sidhis." I still wanted to learn Yogic Flying. Not because I believed that people levitate in the air, and not because I believed in the Maharishi Effect. I understood, at last, that I am a junkie of the inner world. I wanted unbounded peace, but I also wanted the rush of ecstasy.

I sent out an e-mail query to a friend in the Movement who would know about course requirements. I asked for information about upcoming TM-Sidhi courses—scheduling, eligibility, and cost. The reply surprised me more than it should have. Since the last time I inquired, the course fee rose significantly. The cost of the TM-Sidhi program is currently $5,000.

I came to Fairfield to get back on the spiritual path, and I did. I also wanted to find out what happened to the Movement. I did that, too. It is a business.

I phoned Sarah.

"Honey, I'm coming home."

Chapter 16

The Global Country
of World Peace

The religious traditions that I know of all have some way of recognizing spiritual progress. Freemasons give degrees and Roman Catholics confer holy orders.

Maharishi is the only spiritual teacher who gives out report cards. In the Movement, you get real hard numbers that show your level of spiritual attainment vis-à-vis your spouse or employer or neighbor next door.

Whether or not it's a good idea, the Brain Integration Report Card fits in with Maharishi's long-standing desire to make the spiritual scientific. We had something like it in the old days at MIU.

During my first week on campus, before any classes began, all the first-year freshmen took a battery of psychological tests. There were memory tests, tests of cognitive skills, and the granddaddy of them all, the Minnesota Multiphasic Personality Inventory. At the end of the week, I staggered out of the lab feeling like I'd done fifteen rounds in the ring with Muhammad Ali, followed by a lobotomy.

The guy who administered the tests told us that we'd have to take the whole kit and caboodle again at the end of our senior year. They'd compare the results of the two exams and we'd have objective proof of the advantages of Maharishi's Consciousness-Based Education.

The test-taking process was so unpleasant that I held a grudge about it for the whole five years I was at MIU. As my senior year passed, I contemplated the second round of tests with growing horror. If I had to go through the whole miserable business again, at least I'd get the numbers to prove how far I'd evolved.

Like so many of the Movement's best-laid plans, however, the psych exams went nowhere. Graduation day approached with no word of a second round of tests. Apparently I was the only person on campus who remembered the first round.

When it became obvious that I wasn't going to get my progress report, I vowed that I wouldn't leave without getting something in return for the psychological indignities I endured five years earlier.

I marched in to the MIU Psychology Department and told the secretary that I'd like to see my test scores from my freshman year. She was baffled. I explained the whole thing—the MMPI, the plan to do it all again at graduation. She gave me a worried look as she vanished down a hallway into the dim recesses of the Psych wing.

I sat in a chair and waited. Eventually, an important-looking person in a lab coat emerged, walked up to me and, without any preface or explanation, announced:

"Maharishi says that we shouldn't be attached to the fruits of our actions."

He then turned and left.

Decades later, I was still waiting for my score.

I phoned Dr. Travis to inquire about the status of my Brain Integration Report. He said that he couldn't process the data until he received a new piece of software from the National Institutes of Health. I waited a while and phoned again, but he was out of the office for several weeks on the Governor Recertification Course.

I never got my report card.

All that anticipation for . . . what? More numbers. More scores like the ones for Digestive Strength and Ojas Level on my Health and Wholeness Evaluation Report from the Raj.

My brain integration score, if it had ever arrived, would have been a 5 or an 11 or a 98.6 or whatever. I'm still going to have good days and bad days, long dry spells broken by shafts of light. Maybe someday the clouds will lift and I'll wake up for good. If and when that happens, I suppose I won't care much about the numbers. The more I thought about it, the less I cared at all.

Maybe we really shouldn't be attached to the fruits of our actions.

Philosophers of Science put in a good chunk of the last hundred years looking for a reliable method to separate science from pseudoscience. They call this the demarcation problem, and I gather they've largely given up on finding a solution.

With no well-defined yardstick, scientists and the public have to rely on a system of checks and balances to sort productive research from dubious dead ends. It's an imperfect system that sometimes errs against good science, as in the famous case of plate tectonic (continental drift) theory, which most mainstream geologists rejected at first. In the long run, however, the wheat gets separated from the chaff.

For now, at least, the system of checks and balances has kept the Maharishi Effect on the sideline along with other fringe sciences like cold fusion and Intelligent Design. Nothing's set in stone, however. Scientists are willing to throw out the existing paradigm when the evidence is there, as it was for the theory of relativity or quantum mechanics. But science is conservative. In the case of the Maharishi Effect, there are other explanations—coincidence, political and environmental variables, and the preconceptions of the researchers—that we can accept without burning down the house on the off chance that something better might turn up.

Of course, proponents of the Maharishi Effect and other unconventional theories are impatient with the system of checks and balances. It may seem rigid and even prejudiced to them. They may try to avoid the whole process through political action, the courts, or a direct public appeal. Creationists fell back on this strategy to get Intelligent Design into public school classes in Pennsylvania, Kansas, and elsewhere.

That approach seems like a big mistake to me. The system of checks and balances performs such an important function that, in my opinion, it's important to preserve it even though it occasionally flubs.

Think about the consequences of scientific protocol going out the window. This happened to the biological sciences in the Soviet Union in the early part of the twentieth century.

In 1928, an amateur plant breeder named Trofim Lysenko appeared out of nowhere to announce amazing discoveries. Lysenko claimed that his revolutionary techniques would quadruple grain yields and transform the USSR into an agricultural powerhouse.

The Communist Party promoted Lysenko as a hero and the state-controlled media played along by trumpeting Lysenko's few successes and ignoring his many failures. With Stalin's approval, Lysenko rose through the Party hierarchy and took charge of Soviet agriculture.

Once in power, Lysenko launched a series of grand projects to breed new plant species and cultivate new areas of the Soviet empire. When a project bombed, he'd quickly announce something even more amazing.

None of it worked because there wasn't anything to it. "Lysenko-ism," as it's known today, was a strange mixture of folk wisdom, crackpot theories of heredity, and magic. He believed that formal scientific training was unnecessary for success in agronomy. A dedicated plant breeder could create new species on the spot, overcoming any constraints of genetics or Darwinian evolution, through personal willpower and desire.

Russian biologists and geneticists rejected Lysenko's theories from the start, but all they could do was sputter on the sidelines. Lysenko denounced his critics in the scientific establishment as "wreckers" and "people haters." He claimed that they wanted to discredit him out of sour grapes and ruin the Soviet economy in the process. Once again, the media went along and played up the story of the heroic Lysenko versus the treasonous eggheads.

Lysenko got his revenge with Stalin's blessing. Between 1934 and 1940, many Russian geneticists and other scientists were executed or sent to labor camps.

As the crop failures and starvation mounted, Lysenko modified his theories to suit the prevailing winds and made bigger promises. Near the end of his career, with Russian agriculture in ruins, Lysenko proposed his ultimate vision, the Great Stalin Plan for the Transformation of Nature. Fortunately, the Soviet government woke up and put Lysenko under house arrest before he could transform nature any further.

In an open, democratic system such as ours, a Lysenko wouldn't get very far. His kind of dubious science has a much better chance in a closed, authoritarian system. It doesn't have to pass through a gauntlet of checks and balances. It only needs the approval of the big man in charge.

If and when we get a Christian theocracy in the United States, Intelligent Design will sail into the public schools. If the Natural Law Party comes back to win the next presidential election, there will be plenty of federal money for TM and Yogic Flying. Until then, Maharishi will have to abide by the same system of checks and balances as the rest of us.

On October 12, 2000, Maharishi crowned his chief scientist and loyal retainer Dr. Tony Nader, M.D., Ph.D., as His Majesty Raja Nader Raam, First Sovereign of the Maharishi Global Country of World Peace.

The coronation lasted several days. I saw a videotape of the highlights, including the crowning ceremony, which took place in the throne room of Maharishi's house in the Netherlands. Dr. Nader, wearing long gold robes, knelt with his hands pressed together as the wizened guru placed a gold crown on his head. The ceremony concluded in a royal procession with bagpipers, horse-drawn carriages driven by coachmen in livery, an elephant, and, above it all, a small airplane trailing a banner that read:

GLORY TO NADER RAMA, RULER OF GLOBAL COUNTRY

Along with a king, Maharishi's Global Country has a government with forty ministries, which correspond to the forty branches of Vedic literature. His Excellency John Hagelin is Minister of Science and Technology. His Excellency Bevan Morris is Minister of Enlightenment.

Maharishi now offers a Raja Training Course for those "wishing to make an executive career in the administrative service of the Global Country of World Peace." The course fee is $1 million. There are currently about a dozen rajas, each with his own domain, including a Raja of Chicago, a Raja of Atlanta, a Raja of New England, and so forth.

Photos of the coronation appeared on GlobalCountry.org, the official Web page of Maharishi's new country. There was a formal portrait of each raja, in white robe and gold crown, seated on a throne next to his wife in a sari, seated to one side on a lower chair. The captions identified the raja by name but not the wife; e.g., "Raja So-and-So and Wife."

A couple of days after the photos appeared, somebody edited the captions to remove the references to the wives, although the women remained in the photographs. One wag on Fairfield Life asked, "Why don't they just crop them out?"

The Global Country has a flag, a golden sun on a golden background. It has a currency, the Raam Mudra ("money of God"). The exchange rate, which never varies, is one Raam Mudra for ten U.S. dollars.

What the Global Country does not have is territory. It has no laws separating church and state, or any other laws except the Constitution of the Universe—the Vedas. Its citizens, including me, certainly do not have the right to vote. The Maharishi Global Country will continue to exist as long as Maharishi says so, and when he says otherwise, it will pass into the mist.

Chapter 17

A Long, Strange Trip

Three days before my final month's lease ran out, I met Doug for dinner at the old pizza place on the Fairfield square. We gave our order to a middle-aged waitress with an Annette Funicello hairdo.

"Is that the same woman who waited on us twenty years ago?" I asked Doug, who nodded as she came back with our Cokes and iceberg lettuce.

"So you're leaving," he said. "You finally attained escape velocity."

"I was thinking of moving to Fairfield," I said in between spoonfuls of ranch dressing. "I really like it here. It's a very spiritual atmosphere. But I don't think I belong in the Movement, especially if they don't want people like you."

"Hey," he said, "you'd be in good company. A lot of people in this town have either been kicked out of the Movement or they've left in disgust. It's a great support group—it's like they understood what Maharishi wanted to do better than he did.

"There's a rumor going around," he continued. "Maharishi wants us all to go. He knows that we can't become realized as long as we're slaves to the Movement, so he made it so creepy and so expensive that nobody with any sense would stay on."

We raised our Cokes to the people who stayed on the program. The waitress brought our pizza, which was as refreshingly tamasic as the last one we ate at the same table decades ago.

"I guess I came back to Fairfield because I was starved for magic," I said. Then something came to me.

"You can't get rid of magic. It's part of who we are, how we're wired up. If you ignore it or try to get rid of it, it'll come back to haunt you. But we're just as much wired up for reason as we are for magic, and if all you do is magic instead of reason, then . . ."

Doug looked up from his pizza. I thought of the fence along the southern end of campus, King Tony in his gold crown, the Maharishi Effect.

"Well . . . I think reason is at least as important." Doug slurped a thread of mozzarella and nodded, it seemed, without much interest. I realized that he and everybody else in town had probably been through this discussion a million times.

When dessert came, we changed the subject to music. It's good to have a friend like Doug who keeps up with new bands.

After dinner we left the restaurant and walked to the gazebo at the center of the town square. The sun was going down and the first of the teenage cruisers were lining up their Camaros and big-wheeled pickups for the weekly promenade.

"Just like old times," Doug said.

We shook hands and agreed to meet when the Rolling Stones played in Chicago.

His supporters tell you that Maharishi wants to relieve the world's suffering and that everything he does is for that goal. His detractors say that he's in it for wealth and power. Perhaps he started out with the former and wound up with the latter, or perhaps he's had some of both since the beginning.

In any case, I doubt that the fifty years since he left his cave in India have been easy for him. A guru really doesn't have anything resembling a normal life—no friends or coworkers or kids to chill out with at the end of the day. Relationships all go one way, with the guru dispensing from on high and the followers taking it in.

All the checks and balances of everyday life—the little bits of feedback that keep us on track—go out the window. For a guru, it's nonstop praise and devotion. Day after day, a guru hears that he can do no wrong because he's God. After a while, it must be very hard to believe otherwise.

The pressure must be horrible; it's no wonder that so many gurus fall from grace. What's more, a lot of them take the same trajectory as they go. The story is so common that it amounts to a script with the following stages:

1. Innocence. In the beginning, the guru is idealistic and gregarious and available to one and all.
2. Success. When money and fame arrive, the guru becomes less accessible to the rank-and-file faithful.
3. Isolation. The guru retreats into a protective cocoon surrounded by an inner circle of acolytes. The demands for money and obedience increase. The guru's pronouncements become increasingly grandiose and apocalyptic.
4. Bang or whimper. In extreme cases, there's a mass suicide or other tragedy. Usually, though, the guru dies or the group just fizzles out and everybody gets on with their lives.

For all his attempts at innovation, I'd say that Maharishi pretty much stuck to the script. The Movement is currently at stage 3, with everyone waiting on pins and needles to see how stage 4 will transpire.

Some think that Maharishi's passing will mean the end of the Movement, at least in the West. His successors will sell off the MUM property and whatever else is left and cease all activities in the United States and Europe.

Other people assume that an official TM Movement will continue in some form, perhaps under the leadership of John Hagelin or Tony Nader. Of course, neither of them has a fraction of Maharishi's natural charisma and authority. It probably wouldn't be much of a party.

There's also talk of a schism. Perhaps, once the old man is gone, the truly faithful will rally from the shadows and restore the Movement to its pristine glory. No more inflated prices, no more dubious products and services, no more delusions of grandeur. Just sincere individuals teaching Transcendental Meditation to a spiritually hungry world.

Just like old times.

My boxes and bags were packed and my good-byes said. In a few hours, I'd climb into the red convertible and drive out of Fairfield, probably for good this time. However, there was one more place I wanted to visit before I left.

"It's the best thing that ever came out of the Movement."

I heard several variations on that statement from people who were talking about the Maharishi School of the Age of Enlightenment. MSAE is a private school on the MUM campus that caters to the second generation. The parents are Movement people of my cohort—the ones who started TM in the seventies. They came to Fairfield to meditate in the Golden Dome and settled down and got married and had kids—enough kids to support a school based on Maharishi's teachings.

The MSAE Web site proudly notes that "over the past five years the school has averaged about ten times the national average for National Merit Scholar Finalists." MSAE students regularly do well in state and national academic competitions—math exams, science fairs, spelling bees, and writing contests. Oddly enough, given the Movement's general lack of physicality, the school's sports teams often perform well. My favorite MSAE story comes from the parent of a kid on the basketball team.

"Last year our team was playing the team from Ottumwa. Our son talked to one of the Ottumwa kids before the game. The kid said, 'I heard that your team can fly.'"

A casual visitor might assume that the school is the focus of life on the MUM campus. The rest of the university is pretty sleepy, but the school is a beehive of activity. I parked in the jammed lot and followed a group of kids in uniforms—boys in white shirts and ties and girls in green checkerboard dresses—through the single gate of the east-facing fence.

The main building is one of the few left from the original Parsons campus. It felt comfortably lived-in like the grade schools of my memory. I reported to the office and met my guide, an efficient, intelligent woman named Sue who I guessed to be a volunteer parent rather than a Movement employee.

"We really like visitors," she said as she led me down the hallway. "We love showing off."

Our first stop was a grade school class. Sue knocked softly at the door and we slipped in while the kids were practicing their Sanskrit. Sue pointed to the wall and, sure enough, among the maps of the world and the pictures of animals and cloud formations, I saw a poster with the letters of the Sanskrit alphabet.

"All the kids learn Sanskrit as a language requirement," Sue told me as we quietly left the room. "It might seem strange, but it really stands out on a college application. Our kids go to the top colleges—Oxford, Stanford, Smith, Wellesley. Those schools like to see students who have something different on their record. Of course, you've got to have all the regular academic qualifications, too."

Sue took me to a class in Gandharva Veda, or Vedic music. "We make sure they get the whole range of Maharishi's knowledge from the beginning. Ayurveda. Vedic architecture. Vedic mathematics."

We entered a classroom where two students—a boy and a girl I guessed to be around fifteen—sat cross-legged on the floor. Each held a tabla, the Indian hand drum that often accompanies a sitar player.

"Hello, welcome!" said the teacher, a middle-aged Indian man sitting on the floor with his own drum. As we took our places on the floor, Sue introduced me as an old MIU graduate, which brought a happy smile to the teacher's face. He placed his palms together and bowed slightly in my direction and said, "Jai Guru Dev. Would you like to hear some music?"

With his hands and his voice, the teacher led his pupils down a long and twisty path of rhythm. They thumped and stroked their drums as I swayed with the happy music. The girl grimaced briefly over a mislaid beat, but she quickly rejoined the flow with a big grin.

I admired their joy in the music, and I felt a little jealous as I recalled the band classes I endured at their age, bleating out the same Sousa marches over and over until I put down my instrument and never picked it up again. Lucky kids.

"Thank you for visiting our class," the teacher said as Sue and I stood up to leave.

As we walked down a hall to the brahmastan, the center of the building, we encountered a group of little girls in their checkered dresses walking silently in a row.

"They're doing the children's technique," Sue whispered to me. "It's called the word of wisdom. They become eligible for adult TM later on when they're old enough to sit still."

With their teacher in the lead, the line of little yoginis walked silently to the end of the hall, turned around, and walked past us to the other end of the hall, where they turned again. They produced the same atmosphere of silence I felt in the Golden Dome.

Suddenly, I loved them. I loved the little yoginis and I loved the teens playing the tabla. I felt a little bit of moisture form in my eyes.

Our last stop was a class of high school students.

"They're graduating this year," Sue told me. "Almost all our graduates— 95 percent—go on to college. About half enroll at MUM and the rest go to other schools. We figure, if they choose another school, they've grown up in this environment and they want to spread their wings and see the world. That's fine."

We entered the room and Sue had a quick word with the teacher, who instructed the class of perhaps a dozen boys and girls to turn around and greet their visitor.

The students, who were sitting at desks facing away from the door when we entered, stood en masse, picked up their desks, turned them around, sat down again, and looked straight into my soul with eyes as clear as the blue sky. It was the toughest audience I'd ever faced—smart, strong, cool, and able to detect the slightest trace of bullshit. I loved them, but I was a little awed by them, too.

"We have a tradition here," the teacher said. "When a visitor comes to class, the students get to ask questions. I'm sure you'll enjoy it. Does anybody have a question for Mr. Gilpin?"

"What do you do?" asked a boy.

"I'm a writer."

"What do you write?"

"Well, I mainly write computer manuals. But I'm thinking of writing a book about Fairfield and the Movement." And maybe it'll give me a second chance. Maybe, if I tell everybody what happened here, you won't repeat the mistakes we made.

"What was it like when you were a student here?"

"Well . . ." I looked out the window at the sky and the grass of the old quad. I saw the sidewalk that led from the chapel to the student union and the grove of trees where Beth and I discovered a fairy castle.

"Well . . . there wasn't any school back then. Just the university. And none of the meditators lived in town, just on campus. And the knowledge was a lot, well, simpler. There wasn't any Ayurveda. No Vedic architecture or Vedic music. There wasn't anything except Transcendental Meditation."

Several of the kids opened their eyes wide. A couple shook their heads in disbelief and one girl sucked in a deep breath.

"Wow," she said.

Terminology and Characters

The Movement is an informal, umbrella term that encompasses Maharishi Mahesh Yogi, his followers, and the many organizations they've established over the last fifty years. These organizations come and go and, for the most part, few people outside the Movement have heard of them. For instance, many people who learned TM in the sixties and seventies did so under the auspices of a Movement group known as the Students International Meditation Society.

To avoid confusion, I haven't used many formal names for TM organizations in this book. Instead, I've followed the customary practice of lumping it all together as the Movement.

The term Maharishi poses difficulties because it's the title of a particular individual and a trademark that appears on a wide variety of goods and services and organizations. What's more, some people in the TM world use Maharishi and the Movement almost interchangeably. I try to use Maharishi for the man himself unless I specifically name a particular entity, like Maharishi International University, or a set of beliefs or practices, such as Maharishi Architecture.

Some of the formal names and titles in the Movement, like Chairman of the Council of Supreme Intelligence, may sound unusual to some readers. They're recorded accurately. Although I'm not an expert in the matter, my guess is that these names reflect the language and culture of the Movement's founder, Maharishi.

As mentioned in the Preface, some of the characters in this book are composite portraits of two or more real individuals. The most notable composites are the Doug and Beth characters. Also, several of the minor staff characters in scenes set at Movement institutions in Fairfield are composites. Executive Software Decisions is a composite company.

Glossary

Amrit: Nectar.

Ayurveda: The ancient Indian system of traditional medicine. Maharishi Ayurveda refers to trademarked goods and services adapted from traditional Ayurveda.

Brahmachari: One who practices celibacy as a spiritual path.

Brahmastan: The center point of an area such as a building, region, nation, etcetera.

Darshan: The blessing that comes from viewing or being in the presence of an enlightened master; the master's spiritual energy.

Deva: A divine being; a god or deity.

Dhoti: An Indian men's garment consisting of a piece of square cloth wrapped around the body.

Dosha: In Ayurveda, one of the three basic forces, or humors, that govern the body. The doshas are formed from combinations of the five fundamental elements—earth, fire, air, water, and space.

Ghee: Clarified butter used in Indian cooking.

Guru: An exalted spiritual teacher.

Kalash: A pot or pitcher; an ornamental design in architecture.

Kapha: In Ayurveda, one of the three doshas that regulate bodily processes. Kapha is formed from the elements earth and water and governs the structural elements of the body such as the muscles and skeleton.

Karma: Action; the metaphysical law of cause and effect.

Lakshmi: The Indian goddess of wealth and good fortune.

Maharaja: *See* Raja.

Maharishi: *See* Rishi.

Mantra: A sound, word, or phrase used in meditation.

Mudra: A sign, token, or image; a sacred gesture; money.

Pitta: In Ayurveda, one of the three doshas that regulate bodily processes. Pitta is formed from the elements fire and water and governs metabolism and digestion.

Purusha: In Indian religion, the primordial individual who gives rise to creation. Purusha has countless arms, legs, heads, etcetera. Also, the soul or spirit.

Raja: A king. A Maharaja is a great king.

Rakshasa: A demon.

Ram: In Indian religion, an important name of God. Also spelled Rama and Raam.

Rishi: A seer. A Maharishi is a great seer.

Rudraksha: A fruit-bearing tree that grows in India and other parts of Asia. The seeds, also called Rudraksha, are known as Shiva's tears. Necklaces of Rudraksha are worn in India for use in prayer.

Satsang: A gathering of spiritual seekers.

Shiva: In Indian religion, one of the primary trinity of deities, including Brahma and Vishnu. Shiva represents the cosmic principle of destruction that clears the way for a new creation. He is also Lord of Yoga.

Sidha: One who practices sidhis.

Sidhi: A paranormal ability, such as levitation or invisibility, acquired through spiritual practice. Often spelled siddhi.

Tamasic: Impure.

Vata: In Ayurveda, one of the three doshas that regulate bodily processes. Vata is formed from the elements air and space and governs the nervous system and circulation.

Veda: Knowledge, especially of the divine, unchanging Absolute. One of the four foundation texts of Indian religion—the Rig Veda, Sama Veda, Yajur Veda, and Atharva Veda.

Vedic: Of the Veda.

Yama: In Indian religion, the god of death.

Yoga: A system of Indian spiritual practice. The goal of yoga is union with the divine.

Yogi: A male practitioner of yoga.

Yogini: A female practitioner of yoga.

Acknowledgments

Here, at the end of a very long and difficult journey, I look back and offer thanks to the many people who gave aid and comfort along the way.

On the literary front, I'd like to thank Mitch Horowitz, my editor at Tarcher/Penguin, for the vision to believe in this book and the courage to take a chance on its author. Thanks also to my agent, Gail Ross, for her solid professionalism at each step on the path. I'm also deeply grateful to Howard Yoon of the Gail Ross Literary Agency for his hard work and patience.

My friend and fellow memoirist Elena Tabachnick read the manuscript and made many valuable suggestions. Thanks and blessings.

Many current and former members of the Transcendental Meditation Movement generously gave of themselves for this project. First of all, I'd like to thank Maharishi Mahesh Yogi for giving me TM, spiritual direction, and enough material for a dozen books. I'm also thankful to Rick Archer, Kent Boyum, Bob Brigante, Rory Goff, Douglas Hamilton, John Hagelin, Chris Johnson, David Lynch, Ed Malloy, Mario Orsatti, Craig Pearson, Dennis Raimondi, Bob Roth, Fred Travis, Jim Karpen, L.B. Shriver, Keith Wallace, the contributors to the Fairfield Life forum on Yahoo, and the

Fairfield Wednesday night satsang group. To all the rest, I hope you understand how grateful I am.

Many others offered invaluable help with various aspects of this book. Thanks to Professor Malcolm Forster of the University of Wisconsin for his perspective on the philosophy of science, Reverend Scott Prinster of First Unitarian Society in Madison, Wisconsin, for insights on the relationship between science and religion, James "The Amazing" Randi of the James Randi Educational Foundation for his thoughts on magic and skepticism, Professor Emeritus Victor Stenger of the University of Hawaii for help understanding quantum physics, and Professor Kenneth Zysk of the University of Copenhagen for information about Ayurveda.

I began an early draft of this book while I was pursuing a Master of Fine Arts degree in Creative Nonfiction at Goucher College. I'd like to express deep gratitude to my friends and colleagues at Goucher for their help and encouragement. I'm especially grateful to my faculty mentors Philip Gerard, Lee Gutkind, Lisa Knopp, and Leslie Rubinkowski. Thanks also to author Carolyn Kremers for introducing me to the MFA program.

I owe more than I can say to the many friends and family members who kept me going during this long project. Thanks and praises to Leslie Chartier, Martha DiJulius, Beth Genne, Allan Gibbard, Aaron Katcher, Nancy Kremers, Brent McNabb, Ocean Meir, Darrel Richey, Ross Royster, Diana Vezmar-Bailey, and Martha Vincent.

I'd like to thank my mother, Martha Gilpin, for giving me $35 to learn TM. Thank you, also, for a lifetime of inspiration.

Finally, I couldn't have done it without Sarah Cook—friend, companion, lover, editor, and co-conspirator. Yes, love is stronger than fear.

Notes

1. Paul Mason, *The Maharishi: The Biography of the Man Who Gave Transcendental Meditation to the World* (Shaftesbury, Dorset: Element Books Ltd., 1994).

2. www.booksarefunltd.com/whatwedo.aspx.

3. David Orme-Johnson, et al, "International Peace Project in the Middle East: The Effects of the Maharishi Technology of the Unified Field," *Journal of Conflict Resolution,* Vol. 32, No. 4, December 1988.

4. Over the years, the Movement has conducted dozens of research studies on the Maharishi Effect. The Web site for the Maharishi University of Management, www.mum.edu/m_effect/index.html, has a good introduction.

5. www.vedicknowledge.com/Maharishi_effect.html.

6. One of the discussion groups on Yahoo: groups.yahoo.com/group/fairfieldlife.

7. The Thousand-Headed Purusha is the group of celibate monks who devote their lives to serving Maharishi. They are the Jedi Knights of the TM Movement.

8. "Relative," pertaining to the material world as opposed to the transcendent "Absolute."

9. "Meditation is path to peace, Mozambique leader says," *The Guardian* online, September 22, 2001. www.guardian.co.uk/international/story/0,3604,556139,00.html.

10. "Beatles Guru Offers Nirvana to Mozambique," *The New York Times* online archives, February 10, 1994.

11. Large groups of Yogic Flyers.

12. Nancy Lonsdorf, Veronica Butler, and Melanie Brown, *A Woman's Best Medicine: Health, Happiness, and Long Life through Maharishi Ayur-Veda* (New York: Jeremy P. Tarcher/Putnam, 1993), 303.

13. Hari Sharma and Christopher Clark, *Contemporary Ayurveda: Medicine and Research in Maharishi Ayur-Veda* (London: Churchill Livingstone, 1998), 38.

14. www.mvvt.org/index_english.htm.

15. A gathering of spiritual seekers.

16. The term comes from a conference of leading physicists in Denmark in 1927. At the time, there was a lot of debate about features of quantum mechanics—such as the wave/particle duality and Heisenberg's "uncertainty principle"—that seemed to run counter to conventional understandings of mechanics. The "Copenhagen interpretation" is how some of the conference participants attempted to explain these anomalies.

17. Evan Fales and Barry Markovsky, "Evaluating Heterodox Theories," *Social Forces* Vol. 76 (2):511–25, December 1997.

18. Christopher Anderson, "Physicist Running for President is Accused of Distorting Science to Fit Guru's Ideas," *Nature*, Vol. 359, September 10, 1992.

19. "NIH Awards $8 Million Grant to Establish Research Center on Natural Medicine." Quoted from www.mum.edu/inmp/nih.html.

Index

About the Author

Geoff Gilpin lived inside the Maharishi's movement for five years in the 1970s. Gilpin is a computer programmer and technical writer. This is his first work of creative nonfiction. He lives in Wisconsin.